The Rothschild Gardens

The Rothschild Gardens

A Family's Tribute to Nature

Miriam Rothschild

Lionel de Rothschild

Kate Garton

Photographs by

Andrew Lawson

&

Lionel de Rothschild

ABBEVILLE PRESS

NEW YORK   LONDON

LEFT
In spring cherry blossoms frame the steps leading to a mass of cowslips on a once formal lawn at Aston Wold, the author's garden

Published in the United States of America in 2004 by
Abbeville Press, 116 West 23rd Street
New York, NY 10011

First published in paperback in the United Kingdom in 2000
by Gaia Books Limited, 66 Charlotte Street
London W1T 4QE

ISBN: 0-7892-0828-8

Library of Congress information available on request

Set in Goudy

Printed and bound in Hong Kong

2 4 6 8 10 9 7 5 3 1

ACKNOWLEDGEMENTS

First and foremost we must thank Elena Malagodi, Rozsika Parker and Ruth Petrie, for editing and improving the text.

We are most grateful to the various members of the Rothschild family: Beth, Bettina, Edmond, Edmund, Elie, Eric, Guy, Liliane who have greatly assisted us with information and the loan of various old photographs.

Impressive and delightful details were provided by Marcel Gaucher concerning the gardens at Grasse, Boulogne and pre-war Waddesdon, and we are deeply indebted to him for allowing us to read and quote from his copious notes and comments, and for the long afternoon we spent talking to him in his home.

We are indebted to Bob Grace for information about Tring and for the photograph of the Tring gardeners.

We would also like to acknowledge with thanks the assistance we received from The Rothschild Archive, London; the staff of Gunnersbury Park Museum; National Monuments Record Offices at Swindon and London; the owners and managers of the gardens featured in this book; the staff of The Royal Horticultural Society's Lindley Library; the director and his staff at The Royal Botanic Gardens, Kew; Mrs Joyce Stewart; Dr. Phillip Cribb; Sandra Bell; M. Patrick Serier; Hans Dieter Eisterer, Gartenbaumuseum, Vienna; Hugo Trago; Michael McLeod; Dr. A.W. Fried, The Rothschild Foundation, Jerusalem; Ian Hodgkiss; Michael Walker; Arabella Lennox-Boyd; The Bank of England; The Rothschild Archives at Ascott House, Ashton Wold and Exbury; The Rothschild Collection at Waddesdon Manor; The Natural History Museum; The Jewish Museum, Frankfurt-am-Main; Institut für Stadtgeschichte, Stadt Frankfurt-am-Main; Sarah Wilson; Velda Croot; Charlie Ryrie, Gaia Books, for her patience and understanding; June Davies and June Gahan for typing the text.

MIRIAM ROTHSCHILD
KATE GARTON
LIONEL DE ROTHSCHILD
JUNE 1996

Contents

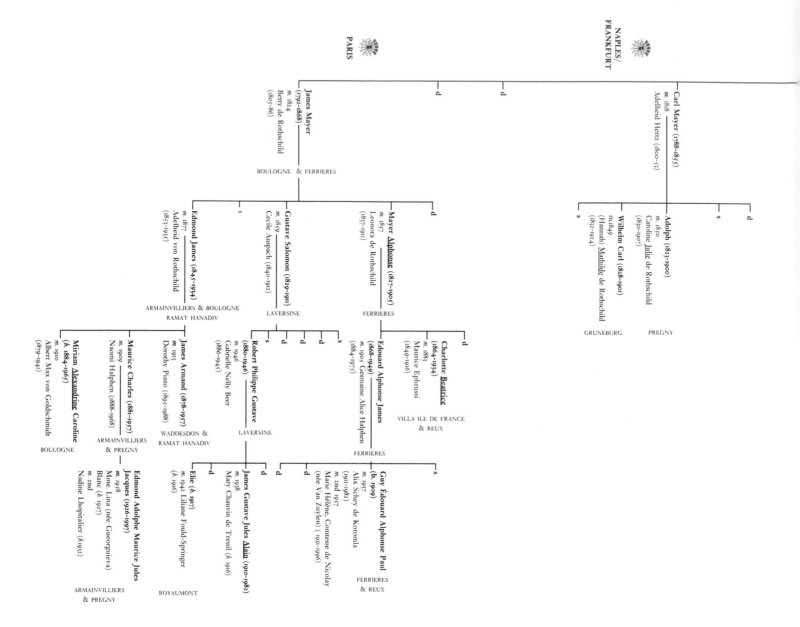

This abbreviated Family Tree shows the principal Rothschild gardeners, with their gardens. Where female Rothschild gardeners married members of the Rothschild family they are shown with their husbands rather than their siblings.

The Rothschild Gardeners

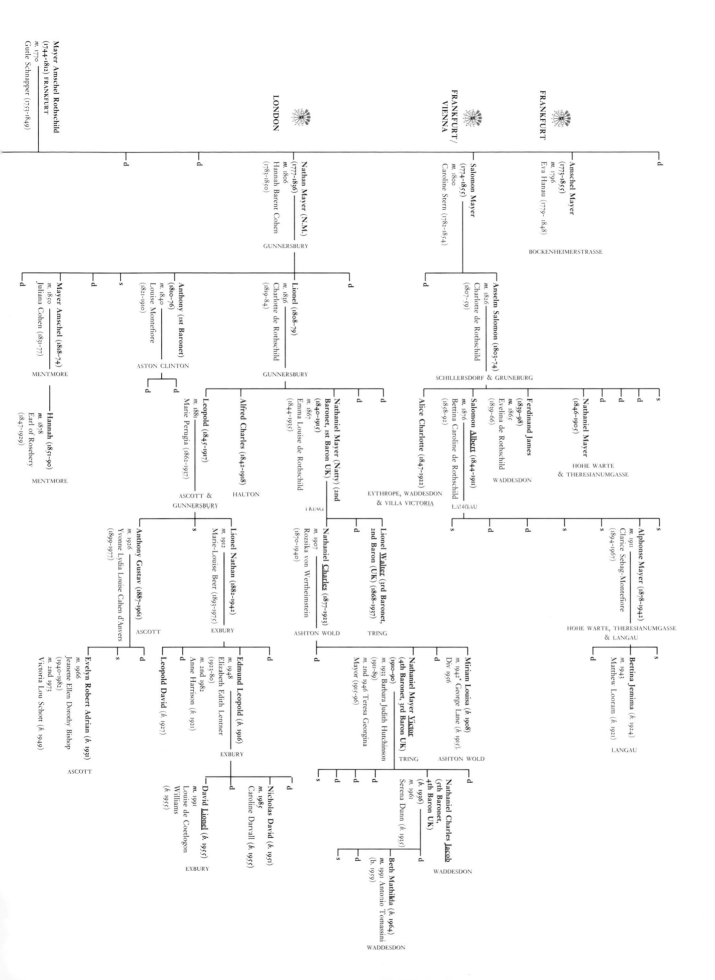

Mayer Amschel Rothschild
(1744–1812) FRANKFURT
m. 1770
Gutle Schnapper (1753–1849)

FRANKFURT

Amschel Mayer
(1773–1855)
m. 1796
Eva Hanau (1779–1848)

BOCKENHEIMERSTRASSE

FRANKFURT/
VIENNA

Salomon Mayer
(1774–1855)
m. 1800
Caroline Stern (1782–1854)

LONDON

Nathan Mayer (N.M.)
(1777–1836)
m. 1806
Hannah Barent Cohen
(1783–1850)
GUNNERSBURY

Anselm Salomon (1803–74)
(1807–59)
Charlotte de Rothschild

SCHILLERSDORF & GRUNEBURG

Nathaniel Mayer
(1846–1905)

HOHE WARTE
& THERESIANUMGASSE

Ferdinand James
(1839–98)
m. 1865
Evelina de Rothschild
(1839–66)
WADDESDON

Salomon **Albert** (1844–1911)
m. 1876
Bettina Caroline de Rothschild
(1858–92)
LANGAU

Alice Charlotte (1847–1922)

EYTHROPE, WADDESDON
& VILLA VICTORIA

Mayer Amschel (1818–74)
m. 1850
Juliana Cohen (1831–77)

MENTMORE

Hannah (1851–90)
m. 1878
Earl of Rosebery
(1847–1929)

MENTMORE

Anthony (1st Baronet)
(1810–76)
m. 1840
Louise Montefiore
(1821–1910)
ASTON CLINTON

Lionel (1808–79)
m. 1836
Charlotte de Rothschild
(1819–84)
GUNNERSBURY

Leopold (1845–1917)
m. 1881
Marie Perugia (1862–1937)
ASCOTT &
GUNNERSBURY

Alfred Charles (1842–1918)
HALTON

Nathaniel Mayer (Natty) (2nd
Baronet, 1st Baron UK)
(1840–1915)
m. 1867
Emma Louise de Rothschild
(1844–1935)
TRING

Lionel **Walter** (3rd Baronet,
2nd Baron (UK)) (1868–1937)
TRING

Nathaniel **Charles** (1877–1923)
m. 1907
Rozsika von Wertheimstein
(1870–1940)
ASHTON WOLD

Alphonse Mayer (1878–1942)
m. 1911
Clarice Sebag-Montefiore
(1894–1967)

HOHE WARTE, THERESIANUMGASSE
& LANGAU

Bettina Jemima (*b.* 1924)
m. 1945
Matthew Looram (*b.* 1921)

LANGAU

Anthony Gustav (1887–1961)
m. 1926
Yvonne Lydia Louise Cahen d'Anvers
(1899–1977)
ASCOTT

Lionel Nathan (1882–1942)
m. 1912
Marie-Louise Beer (1892–1975)
EXBURY

Miriam Louisa (*b.* 1908)
m. 1942* George Lane (*b.* 1915),
Div 1976
ASHTON WOLD

Nathaniel Mayer **Victor**
(4th Baronet, 3rd Baron UK)
(1910–90)
m. 1933 Barbara Judith Hutchinson
(1911–89)
m. 2nd 1946 Teresa Georgina
Mayor (1915–96)
TRING

Nathaniel Charles **Jacob**
(5th Baronet,
4th Baron UK)
(*b.* 1936)
m. 1961
Serena Dunn (*b.* 1935)
WADDESDON

Evelyn Robert Adrian (*b.* 1931)
m. 1966
Jeanette Ellen Dorothy Bishop
(1940–1982)
m. 2nd 1973
Victoria Lou Schott (*b.* 1949)
ASCOTT

Leopold David (*b.* 1927)

Edmund Leopold (*b.* 1916)
m. 1948
Elizabeth Edith Lentner
(1923–86)
m. 2nd 1982
Anne Harrison (*b.* 1921)
EXBURY

David **Lionel** (*b.* 1955)
m. 1991
Louise de Coetlogon
Williams
(*b.* 1955)

Nicholas David (*b.* 1951)
m. 1985
Caroline Darvall (*b.* 1955)

Beth Matilda (*b.* 1964)
m. 1991 Antonio Tomassini
(*b.* 1959)

WADDESDON

Preface

No attempt has been made to compile a Catalogue of the Rothschild gardens or the plants they grew in them, since - taking into account the smaller houses the family have built or acquired - they must number over a hundred. We decided, as authors, to select a few of the gardens and parks we knew best and liked most, and have "wandered round them", not attempting to produce accurate plans of the layouts and cultivations of the competent head gardeners who worked for the owners.

Yet it is with great regret that through lack of space gardens like those of Schillersdorf, Grüneburg, Aston Clinton, Mentmore and the various town gardens are merely referred to in passing.

All three authors shared the research involved but the major contribution to this part of the book has been made by Kate Garton. I have written the text except for the chapter on Exbury, which is the work of Lionel de Rothschild.

It is most unfortunate that colour photography was in its infancy when the Rothschild gardeners were producing their blaze of gaudy flowers, which leaves a serious gap in our records – for photographs bring life to these descriptions.

A quick survey of the Rothschild gardens, past and present, brings home to us the easily forgotten and overlooked minor disasters and the senseless destruction of war and human folly. But curiously enough the post-war redistribution of wealth, both in Europe and the United States, has produced a widespread and greatly enhanced interest in the cultivation of flowers and the creation of gardens. There are more horticultural centres in England today, and a greater interest in the native flora than ever before. Can we be more optimistic about the future of the green world?

MIRIAM ROTHSCHILD
Ashton Wold, June 1996

RIGHT
Wild flowers in a Rothschild
garden, grown from seeds
supplied by the author

Part One

The Rothschild Gardens

ONE

A Passion for Gardening

"A necessity as much as bread"
NATHAN MAYER ROTHSCHILD

It is a melancholy fact that writings about gardens, whether in prose or poetry, have much in common with anthologies of love letters. The authors themselves may find the repetitive endearments and the interminable descriptions of scented roses and varieties of apples delightful, full of moving memories, poetry and joy, but the uninvolved reader can find them all remarkably similar, a trifle meaningless and repetitive. It requires considerable courage to put pen to paper in praise of gardens. Furthermore, they themselves are frighteningly ephemeral and with change of ownership go out like a light.

It is not merely that a new proprietor may decide to dig up the beds of flowers and replace them with neat serried rows of onions, but both Nature and variation in human character and taste work inexorably together to initiate and ensure change. Sometimes, in a "stately home", where the framework remains, the new generation of gardeners, restrained by tradition and familiarity, are successful in perpetuating the previous scene. But this is rare. The two World Wars have also proved profoundly destructive.

The Rothschild gardens usually survived two, sometimes three, generations. But they were unique, since between 1850 and 1914 they spanned England, France, Germany, Austria and Switzerland with many notable creations. The majority of these were characteristic of the late Victorian/Edwardian era, when a mixture of formal design with exuberant planting of flowers and trees was fashionable. All the Rothschilds were enthusiastic devotees of heated glasshouses and the propagation of exotic plants, especially tropical orchids and luxury fruit.

PREVIOUS PAGES
The restored parterre at
Waddesdon Manor
with Beth Rothschild

RIGHT
Flamboyant parterres typify
the Rothschild passion
for Edwardian-style
garden design

They were also dedicated collectors, whether of classical works of art, fleas, books, autographs, thimbles, butterflies, *têtes-de-mort*, Sèvres porcelain, postage stamps or shotguns. In their gardens they collected rhododendrons[1] and iris species and endless varieties of decorative plants. Edmond at Boulogne and Lionel at Exbury became noted horticulturalists, experimenting with crosses of carnations, arums, orchids and rhododendrons and propagating orchids by advanced laboratory methods, while my father Charles was an excellent botanist, interested in wild flora and their conservation. His collection of irises and orchids went to Kew on his death. It was my mother Rozsika who was the traditional gardener at Ashton.

The family as a whole loved trees as well as smaller plants. "Natty", the first Lord Rothschild, planted blue spruce in the misnamed Elizabethan garden at Tring, which attained gigantic proportions. In the park near Wigginton, he created a small arboretum of fir trees – a great variety of interesting species – and he kept a flock of albino peacocks in this area. As a child, I was spellbound by their beautiful display seen against a background of black-green fir trees. One of the great attractions of Ashton for Charles was the mile-long avenue of 200 old elms, planted about 1730, which, quaintly, led from nowhere to nowhere.

The family liked to see kangaroos, various deer, emus, rheas, ornamental pheasants and peacocks in their parks, tropical birds in the aviaries and tropical fish and salamanders in the heated tanks. As travelling had become relatively easy various members of the family sent collectors abroad to find rare and interesting plants for their gardens. They were also determined to improve everything and produce excellence by able management. Natty was just as keen to increase the milk output of his Jersey cows as the size and colour of his yellow Malmaison carnations and the apples in the orchard at Dundale.

On account of their large houses, art collections, luxurious gardens and beautiful parks, the Rothschilds were accused of ostentation and apeing the aristocracy, and thus advertising their rise from struggling Jewish merchants to persons of consequence and considerable power. There may well have been some truth in these ill-natured criticisms[2]. They were certainly highly competitive and keen to win distinction, for instance at horticultural flower shows. But most of their rivalry was rather childishly directed at other members of the family, not the outside world. Nevertheless, a letter to her mother-in-

ABOVE
Alice de Rothschild, the most talented Rothschild gardener, nicknamed by Queen Victoria "the All Powerful"

ABOVE RIGHT
Spring bedding in the parterre at Waddesdon

BELOW RIGHT
Kangaroos in the park at Tring

law survives in which Emma – Natty's cousin and wife – finishes her paean of praise of Blenheim and its treasures by commenting that "the grapes were not nearly as fine as those grown at Gunnersbury". But the real motive and stimulus behind the Rothschilds' gardens and parks was quite simple – they truly loved flowers.

This love of plants and animals was already in evidence in the Frankfurt ghetto[3]. The house in Jew Street, where Amschel Mayer lived with his parents from 1773 to 1812 was small and cramped. All ten children shared one tiny bedroom. His mother cooked for her large family in a passage (5 feet by 12 feet) in which there was room for only one pot on the hearth. It was a miracle that Amschel Mayer found room on the balcony – which overlooked the yard and was called "the terrace" – to cultivate his garden of pot plants on which he lavished almost fanatical care and attention. It is strange to recall that his great-nephew Leopold's exhibit of flowers and fruit, at the Royal Horticultural Society's Show at Chelsea 150 years later, occupied a floor space sixteen times that of the first Rothschild banking house in the Frankfurt ghetto.

Amschel Mayer was the eldest son of the family, but he was childless, and took a less active part in the Rothschild business than his four brothers. In middle age he decided to buy himself a house in the suburbs, with a garden which terminated in a small park. He consulted Nathan when about to make the purchase and found his brothers exceedingly worried. They feared that such signs of "luxurious living" would stimulate anti-Semitic outbursts in the press. Nathan, from England, wrote: "Do not buy a house, wait until my accounts are straight. As far as a garden is concerned I am in full agreement with you buying one as it is for health reasons and can be looked upon as a necessity just as much as bread. But, we are definitely against a house." The brothers changed their minds.

A year later Carl was sending Amschel flower seeds "brought by Humboldt from Africa. These should be planted in pots in February and as soon as the cold nights are gone, put out into the open; very beautiful autumn flowers these are, which have not been sent so far out of Africa."[3] The younger brothers never failed to remember plants for Amschel's garden when they were trading with distant countries. Even when the cargoes of merchandise were large and difficult, they managed somehow. On one occasion the transport of nine horses by sea proved particularly troublesome, but the plants received special

ABOVE
*Nathan Mayer Rothschild –
"a necessity as much as bread"*

attention and, "for fear they should perish", were forwarded by mail coach from France.

Amschel, despite all the hazards, persuaded a number of people to collect for him in foreign lands. The head gardener of the Court of Bavaria wrote to Nathan Mayer in 1819: "I beg to inform you that I arrived here [Rotterdam? En route to Frankfurt] only on the 30th with the plants. The *Erica* have been completely destroyed by the seawater. My lodgings were a sailor's hole and I was about to perish from misery and hunger. Because it is too early to buy bulbs at Harlem....I did not purchase any".[3] *Erica* seems to have been an unlucky *genus*, for in another letter a firm writes (to N.M.): "We found in packing the plants this morning that our packers left out of the package *Erica grandiflora* as the carpenter had made the box too small."

Amschel wrote happily about his garden: "It is a veritable paradise, and is very big, there is room for large families [of plants]." He thanked his brothers enthusiastically: "Your three plants arrived yesterday and gave me great joy, all in good conditions. I am very grateful, and I wish that all of us could enjoy them in a thousand years time and later still."

Bismarck dined with Amschel Mayer and wrote to his wife describing the superb little garden and "the real old Jew pedlar, who does not pretend to be anything else." He noted that during dinner the servant was ordered to take some bread to the tame deer. Amschel Mayer also offered the Baron one of his plants, which he said had cost him two thousand gulden. Eventually, Bismarck left with a few leaves from the plant in question, which he enclosed in the letter to his wife. It is strange that a man born and reared in the Frankfurt ghetto and descended from a Jewish community totally removed from the countryside and any form of horticulture and gardening, should have spontaneously developed, as a young boy, such an enduring love of plants and flowers. Furthermore, there was no one to guide and instruct him and later he deplored his ignorance: "I am not even an amateur and do not understand anything of it."

An affinity with nature and what the great biologist E.O. Wilson[4] called "the secure biophilic pleasure from the propinquity of growing plants" must surely be the expression of an inherited gene – a gene for an aesthetic and highly developed interest in the natural world. It is not difficult to envisage its evolutionary advantage in the past history of the human race.

This characteristic was manifest at an early age in subsequent generations of the Rothschild family. For instance, in an otherwise unbearably critical diary[3], Charlotte comments on her son's educational progress thus: "Natty continues to take great interest in botany, agriculture, the natural history of domestic animals.....he superintends the arrangement of the stables and of the farm, and the kitchen garden; the orchard, the green and hothouses claim his attention and he understands these matters perfectly well." He was then 16. Natty eventually read botany at Cambridge University. Charlotte encouraged this study because "the pursuit of it takes my son into the open air and gives him wholesome invigorating exercise". Charlotte herself made a fine collection of hothouse orchids. The catalogue she compiled contained 94 worldwide species.[5]

It is remarkable that individual Rothschilds, in the long run, proved more faithful to gardening than to banking. Sir Anthony at Aston Clinton, and Mayer at Mentmore, were not able financiers and spent little time at New Court, but they created beautiful gardens. This may well have been due to the fact that their wives – especially those who were born Rothschilds – assumed a more active role in planning their *parterres* than in their financial operations. Hannah (who was N.M. Rothschild's wife and not born a Rothschild) was the exception who did both.

Owing to the destruction of the two World Wars[6], not only a number of the gardens were lost, but also the bulk of papers relating to them, including all the drawings and plans. Their origins are mostly shrouded in mystery. At both Ferrières and Tring there was a minimum of neat flower beds surrounding the main residence, and the very beautiful parks rolled away from the terraces; much the same could be said of the designs of Mentmore and Pregny. Paxton built both the houses and laid out the parks at Ferrières, Pregny, Mentmore, Boulogne and Aston Clinton. At Tring, the park had remained untouched since the early eighteenth century; only the two stretches of water had been drained before Lionel de Rothschild bought it in 1872. Edmond, Natty and Mayer specialised in flowers and fruit grown in extensive hothouses and also planted various groups of trees in the parks. They all had a weakness for blue spruce.

Pregny was the one outstanding Rothschild property in Switzerland and the park was essentially the creation of Paxton and

ABOVE
Lionel de Rothschild who bought Tring for his son "Natty"

RIGHT
Map of Gunnersbury Park, with geological sections and views taken on the Estate, London 1847
Reproduced with kind permission of
The Royal Collection
© Her Majesty The Queen

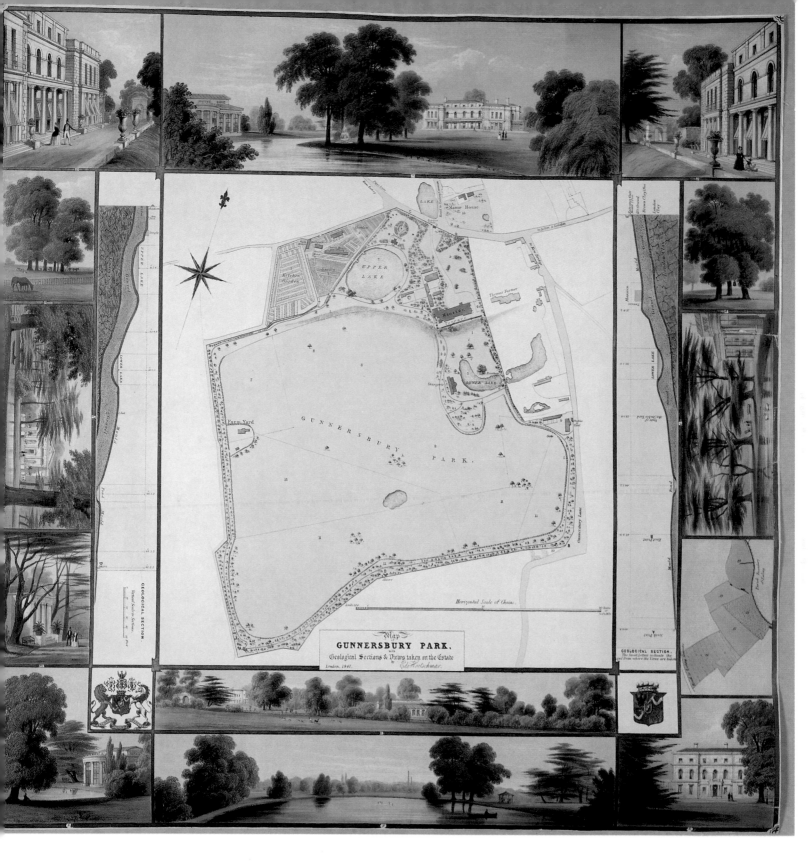

Map
GUNNERSBURY PARK,
with
Geological Sections & Views taken on the Estate
by Edw. Hoolschmar.

London. 1847.

Julie (1830–1907), Baron Adolph's wife and cousin, who was something of a genius and whose taste spanned three generations.

I do not believe any Rothschild before 1940 dug, planted, weeded, pruned, took cuttings, spread straw on the strawberries or even watered their plants. They planned and directed all the arrangements, from the lawns to the Japanese gardens and lily ponds, selected the plants and trees, acquired a wide knowledge and understanding of them, took infinite trouble in procuring the right soil and mixtures for the different projects, and found the right head gardener and staff. They built up small relevant libraries and carried on voluminous correspondence with their collectors and fellow gardeners, and employed a wide range of seed merchants, nurserymen, growers, importers, and florists who supplied them with horticultural varieties, novelties and rarities. They sometimes experimented and carried out various hybridisations. But, they did not indulge in manual labour. This was basically a question of time. For instance, my father corresponded with 60 iris specialists all over the world but he made it a rule never to deal with his garden and his entomological studies between 9 a.m. and 5 p.m. while he was at his desk at N.M. Rothschild & Sons. He was far too busy during his "spare time" collecting insects and recording wild plants to spend his weekends digging or mowing.

At the turn of the century the Rothschild gardens reached their maximum size, varying from six acres at Ashton to 135 hectares at Grasse, where Alice employed over 100 gardeners at the Villa Victoria and each year planted 55,000 daisies, 25,000 pansies, 10,000 wallflowers, 5,000 forget-me-nots, 23,000 bulbs of various sorts, tulips, narcissi and so forth.

From Gunnersbury, a drawerful of invoices survived from Leopold's day, illustrating the size of his enterprise. One purchase included six tons of fibrous loam, four tons of coconut fibre, five yards of oak and beech mould and 50 yards of leaf and peat mould. Other invoices record orders for 300 yews, 68 hollies, 50 lilacs, poplars, ash, lime, pine, sycamore, plane trees and copper beech; there were also annual consignments of flowering plants such as 2,500 lily-of-the-valley (of which 1,500 were "retarded"), 800 Sternbergia and 112 dwarf roses.

For Alexandrine's garden at Boulogne (which she inherited from her father Edmond) her gardener was told to obtain, for example, among many other species, 67 varieties of sweet peas (1,700 plants)

ABOVE
*Alexandrine de Rothschild, who grew
67 varieties of sweet peas*

RIGHT
*Sweet peas growing in a Rothschild
garden today*

LEFT
A plant of Phalaenopsis grown at Tring by Walter Rothschild

BELOW
An exuberant display of hothouse orchids

RIGHT
Tring gardeners dressed for a wedding

and ten varieties of geraniums (39,275 plants). All these were carefully arranged according to colour. In her father's day the garden produced 150,000 pot plants every year.[7]

Although there is no doubt that the most successful part of the Rothschild gardens were their hothouses, with the exotic flowers, creepers, cacti, palms and wide range of fruit which they grew under glass, each garden also contained rare and interesting species, especially orchids. Walter, at Tring, discovered that a light frost in winter enhanced the flowers of certain species of *Vanda* and he succeeded in growing *Phalaenopsis*[8] with an unusual number of branched sprays. One of the plants carried 104 flowers in bloom.

At the Royal Horticultural Society's shows between 1889 and 1913, Rothschilds won 374 awards with, for example hippeastrums, blue waterlilies, orchids, pelargoniums, lobelia, rhododendrons, white crinum, moss roses, fruit trees, alpine strawberries, figs, melons, apples, pears and nectarines, grapes, and so on.

Today, air travel and the freezing techniques available have removed the wonder and delight – and their delicious delicate flavours – of such fruit as pineapples, figs and nectarines grown in one's own garden. These can now be bought on stalls and shops on every street, but in Victorian and Edwardian epochs were a great and rare luxury.

Their gardens were probably the Rothschilds' most expensive hobby, despite the fact that in the last century labour was available at relatively low wages. Nathan (now "his accounts were straight"!) left his widow an annuity of £20,000, which today would have the purchasing power of £880,000. Hannah could, therefore, afford to create a beautiful garden in which she entertained many distinguished guests and romped with her grandchildren.

Alice, (who inherited Waddesdon from her brother in 1898), spent approximately £7,500 on the gardens and £6,200 on the grounds and plantations annually. These figures did not include expenditure on painting and general repairs to the glasshouses, nor on the tools and implements. The biggest extravagance, apart from the gardens, was on the farm and dairy, which cost £4,168. In 1907, the purchasing power of one pound was equal to £44 today, and thus

BELOW
At the Villa Victoria at Grasse, Alice's gardens included this "magnificent grassplot perfumed with flower bulbs, an infinite variety of narcissi, jonquils, tulips, anemones and hyacinths"

Alice was spending well over half a million pounds each year in our currency on the garden and grounds. In addition she invested £2,000 during the same period in the Eythrope garden and grounds, including embellishment of the river bank. Unfortunately, all the accounts relating to the Villa Victoria were lost during the Second World War, but one must conclude the cost of the gardens at Grasse in 1907 considerably exceeded that of Waddesdon and Eythrope combined, and in today's currency Alice – who had no family – spent over a million pounds annually on her gardens. These were her children.

At the turn of the century, the post of head gardener at a Rothschild garden was one of great responsibility and required knowledge, skill and enterprise. Today he or she must also know something about marketing, but that was not required at Waddesdon until after the Second World War. Alice, during her reign, acquired two of the family's most distinguished gardeners, Marcel Gaucher in France and G.F. Johnson in England. They each spent some time working in her

BELOW
Grapes in a greenhouse at Eythrope, home of the present Lord Rothschild

gardens in both countries. After her death, Marcel Gaucher's father, and then he himself, were employed by Edmond at Boulogne and Armainvilliers. Here again the joint staff consisted of 100 men and the garden at Boulogne covered 30 hectares. After Edmond's death, he remained there with Alexandrine until the outbreak of war.

I was fortunate to have known both these superlative gardeners and was able to obtain from Gaucher his opinion, which was both shrewd and perceptive, of his two principal employers. He emphasised the fact that the enormous garden at Grasse was bought piecemeal by Alice, in small lots, and it was entirely her creation, while Edmond's father, James, had laid out the garden at Boulogne before him. He pointed out that Alice was a spinster with a taste for authority, gifted with a high I.Q., an astonishing memory and a terribly autocratic personality. She had fallen in love with the Mediterranean flora in 1887 and thereafter spent six months of the year (October to March) on the Riviera. He considered her a born landscape gardener, a passionate botanist with an exceptional eye for the design of garden arrangements, and she herself ferretted out the finest specimens of trees and plants, which she discovered in various nurseries and horticultural centres, and for which she paid top prices.

Marcel Gaucher mentioned the aprocryphal tale that during Queen Victoria's visit to the Villa, named in her honour, Alice peremptorily ordered her off a corner of the garden for fear of her trampling upon some rare and precious plant – after which the Queen nicknamed her "the All Powerful".

Although Baron Edmond was 83 years old while he himself was only 22, from the first moment Gaucher was drawn to him by a feeling of respectful devotion, and quickly abandoned the job he had in mind and entered the Baron's service. He described their walks together, when the Baron stopped at intervals and examined the flowers at leisure, asking penetrating questions – profoundly interested in botanical details. At these times, said Gaucher, it was fascinating to listen to him. At the end of his life Edmond preferred the simple flowers of the fields to his magnificent hothouse plants and he allowed the grass to grow naturally in certain parts of the garden. He manifested spontaneous delight if he discovered a species new to him. He liked walking in long grass and once stopped an old retainer, conscientiously sweeping up the leaves, because he liked the feel of them beneath his feet. "The first impression of the Baron", said Gaucher,* "was quite extraordinary. He looked so kind, his eyes were so blue, and his long silvery hair, slightly waved, gave his face an appearance of singular nobility".

When Hannah de Rothschild was attempting to further her husband, Lord Rosebery's political career, she decided that her role must be that of a successful hostess[9]. Similarly, to further their husbands' and sons' careers as eminent bankers, other Rothschild wives followed the same course. Adept at taking care of every detail, and in the arrangement of sumptuous receptions, great attention was paid to the floral decorations of the rooms and tables, and in particular, to the fruit and vegetables served at luncheons and dinners. I still remember from my childhood the azaleas, growing in huge Chinese *cache-pots*, which greeted guests arriving in the hall at Tring; a cascade of bright pink flowers completely hid every leaf from view. These floral arrangements and the vases containing sprays of *Oncidium* and fountains of carnations, so impressed me by their beauty, that I never forgot the name of "Mr Keene", the expert member of the garden staff who was responsible for the floral decorations.

Marcel Gaucher gave me a graphic description of the cultivation of fruit for Edmond's households in Paris and Boulogne. He explained that the Baron required fruit spread over an unnaturally long season, for example the first ripe cherries from the glasshouse had to be served by the 1st April. This entailed careful management in a range especially constructed for forcing fruit, and the selection of different varieties, some ripening early, some late. Pollination proved a problem until beehives were installed in the hothouses. Edmond, who had a great appreciation of the beauty of these little trees, liked his guests to be able to pick their fruit at dinner. Dwarf trees in pots were produced with great skill and expertise, laden with ripe red and black cherries or miniature greengages, and were offered during the dessert course. Gaucher remarked that it was a beautiful sight to see the cherry trees in full bloom through the glasshouses when it was snowing outside.

He also grew 3,000 strawberries in pots to produce fruit over a prolonged period, forcing them in a hothouse in series of 500 plants, then cooling them in a cold house and passing them through ether vapour to curb the rise of sap. When ripe, fruit had to be served with great care, stalks uppermost, to make it easier for guests to select and handle each strawberry. Only a special member of his staff was allowed to arrange them in little blue-lined baskets; it was a rigid rule that no servant was allowed to touch fruit for the table – only the gardener.

In his clear handwriting Gaucher entered in one of his note-books varieties of 33 cherries, 40 peaches, 46 pears, 37 apples, 12 plums, nine vines, 24 blackberries and four strawberries at Boulogne. Besides his fruit and vegetables, he also produced mushrooms in two whitewashed cellars, all the year round, except in the hottest summer months. He harvested two to three kilos every morning.

Inevitably, owing to the vagaries of ripening, there was often a surplus of fruit at Boulogne and Edmond took immense pleasure surprising his friends with a box of grapes or nectarines. In addition, about 60 dozen such boxes were distributed annually to hospitals and old folks homes.

The staff at all the Rothschild gardens numbered among them a fully trained packer. The boxes were made of light unstained wood, and when fruit was despatched, were lined with fresh vine leaves. For peaches, a thin layer of sheeted cotton wool was added. Pristine tissue paper protected the dew-fresh flowers and fruit that miraculously – or so it seemed – avoided even a hint of bruising or crushing. Recipients of such boxes were astonished and delighted; they were an enchanting and memorable detail of the whole enterprise.

RIGHT
*Roses climb up the walls and wild flowers grow
in beds below in this greenhouse at
Ashton Wold, home of the author*

FOOTNOTE

* *Marcel Gaucher gave a somewhat similar account in his book Les Rothschild: Côté jardins, 1982*

Part Two

Glorious Gardens

~ ~ ~

TWO

Waddesdon Manor

Most fortunately the National Trust decided (in 1958) to restore the garden at Waddesdon to what it was in Ferdinand and Alice's day[1]. Therefore one typical Rothschild garden will remain, since neither Exbury nor Ashton are "typical", and the Villa Ile de France has become virtually the setting of Beatrice's delightful Museum. The fact that Lord Rothschild's daughter Beth, who trained at the Royal Botanical Gardens at Kew, is available to supervise the reconstruction, is even more fortunate. Restoration of the garden and grounds (165 acres) is a daunting project and certain modern features are also being added. It is an ongoing programme which will bring Waddesdon forward into the next century.

The creator of Waddesdon was Ferdinand – an Austrian great grandson of Mayer Amschel – a melancholy widower whose wife and unborn son died following a railway accident, a blow from which he never really recovered. To drown his sorrows he threw himself with almost frantic zest and energy into building the Manor and creating the garden on 2,700 acres of bare hilltop in the Vale of Aylesbury - a veritable *tour de force*[2]. As a child I was told that Ferdinand had even bred a special strain of powerful Percheron horses in order to transplant full-grown trees to the site chosen for the Manor. The telegraph poles and wires, so they said, had to be moved to allow the enormous trees to be drawn along the village High Street by a team of 20 horses.

Even as a schoolgirl and a frequent visitor to Waddesdon, at a time when my cousins James and Dorothy were living there, I was aware of a subtle air of melancholy which seemed to float above the garden. I attributed this to a certain sense of incongruity – a French château overlooking

PREVIOUS PAGES
The statue of Eros stands behind a carpet of tulips at Ascott in spring

RIGHT
The central pool on the terrace at Waddesdon, its fountain sculpted by Mozani

the Vale of Aylesbury; but since the restoration has taken place this feeling has vanished like mist before the sun. Furthermore the freak 1987 gale, which engendered such devastation at Tring and Ashton, provided a fortunate accident at Waddesdon, for the conifers, especially the spruce and cedars, had grown so luxuriously they had formed a solid shroud of dark green gloom round the house and garden. This was especially striking between the entrance gates and the front door, where the house seemed to be sleeping in deep mourning. The trees were miraculously thinned out by the gale and now form an ideal background for the dazzling *parterres*.

Like so many members of his family, Ferdinand loved animals, especially his dog. He housed llamas and Sika deer in paddocks near the main entrance, and there were emus in a pen and a mountain goat in the rockery. Ferdinand probably employed his architect Destailleur[3] to construct the graceful, white-painted metal aviary in which he kept a large selection of brilliantly coloured tropical birds. I presented a pair of Rothschild Grackles to the aviary in 1954, since only about 40 pairs of this extremely rare bird still exist in the wild on the Island of Bali, and I hoped we might increase their numbers by breeding them in captivity. Unexpectedly, this proved most successful. At that time, James kept snowy owls in the aviary and also my black-headed gulls, in addition to tropical species.

Ferdinand employed Halliday's of Manchester to design and build his 50 greenhouses; these were replaced with modern glass by James in the thirties.

Originally the terrace was the *pièce de resistance*. It followed the English fashion of those days – a pool with a fountain sculpted by an Italian artist, Mozani, in the centre – to the right and left flamboyant *parterres*; a bright golden yew hedge surrounded by a stone balustrade with statues of goddesses at the corners, and urns full of flowers at intervals along the parapet.

The restoration began in 1989. During the Second World War the parterres (like my mother's rose beds at Ashton) were grassed over and grew vegetables. It was difficult to decide exactly which beds were to be used in the restoration since the original shapes had been altered

RIGHT
Waddesdon in autumn

or lost as time went on. One pattern was eventually chosen which permitted the use of modern mowers for the strips of grass round the beds – probably cut by hand in the good old days. In order to ensure the maintenance of the chosen lines, steel plates were inserted along the edges. Drastic reduction of the topiary and the yellow and green yews had to be undertaken, since they had grown to an enormous size and the dividing line between the two colours had been lost. Fortunately today yew clippings are of pharmacological interest and their collection and dispatch is well organised.

Before planting could be envisaged the soil was cleaned by steam sterilisation and an automatic irrigation system installed. This consisted of a system of underground pipes linked to pop-up sprinklers placed at regular intervals throughout the terrace, carefully concealed by turf; each station can be isolated and the water directed in larger quantities to sunny patches – this also allows for feeding with liquid seaweed extract from underground tanks. No doubt in Ferdinand's day watering was done by hand, from hoses affixed to standpipes installed at regular intervals and with watering cans.

The drainage had to be repaired and plastic pipes replaced the worn iron ones, now over 100 years old. Miraculously the original chambers were still in good condition. Path surfaces in the terrace were replaced with hoggin, their original surfacing, and some heavy machinery (J.C.B.s and dumper trucks) had to be used in the process. In Johnson's day as head gardener there were 53 garden staff at Waddesdon, and today the restoration is undertaken by nine, including Beth, but this drastic reduction is possible only because of the machinery now available. A sample of the modern equipment in use is appended (*see p. 46*).

Modern equipment is also used in the aviary – broody bantams are delights of the past. Today they are replaced with electronic incubators and brooders incorporating highly accurate thermostats. These even allow hand-rearing of parrot chicks where temperature control is critical. It is now known that by extending the photo-period, birds will eat more and their increased body heat improves their condition during the winter months. This is achieved with electric lighting, and dimmers are used to give a false dawn and dusk.

The statues, fountains, carved urns and various carved vases and stone containers were fashionable in Ferdinand's day and a very large collection of copies of goddesses and muses (on pedestals of pink

RIGHT
Geraniums blooming in one of the many
greenhouses at Eythrope

Sienna marble designed by Destailleur) were much admired by visitors to Waddesdon. These entail a lot of care and attention: for instance all are cleaned and painted annually with a biocide, and in the winter swathed in anti-frost protectors. Considerable repairs were required to the sculptures, jets of water had to be realigned and fountain pumps repaired. Fortunately the gardens are laid out on such a generous scale that the statues are not too close together (as they were at Halton) and the "museum" atmosphere entirely avoided.

Planting of the terrace *parterres* proved a difficult enterprise. Ferdinand used only annuals, many of them tender species, and replanted two or three times during the summer with potted plants in flower, grown under glass. The mop-headed bay trees were grown in wooden boxes which were then sunk and concealed under the turf, but returned to the greenhouses in winter. For yellow foliage golden pyrethrums were used while house leeks provided lines of silver. In addition there was a spring bulb display surrounded by forget-me-nots.

Today this *régime* is simply not practicable. It was decided on a combination of 25,000 annuals and perennials (*see p. 42*). Spring

BELOW
The Rothschild Grackle

bedding uses a total of 75,000 bulbs and annuals; the choice of plants proved so difficult that a two-year trial was carried out in the beds on either side of the fountain. Some modern plants have now been used. 'Alex' is an infant strain of 'Paul Crample', a scarlet geranium from the original Waddesdon flowerbeds; about 9,000 were planted on the terrace in 1996 and another 650 in the conservatory, in stone vases and in beds on the south front.

There are of course inevitable problems arising from squirrels, badgers, rabbits, Muntjac deer and helminths in a garden open to woodland. All Rothschild gardeners were tree lovers and certainly at Waddesdon they occupied considerably more acreage than flowers. Great attention was paid to especially strong, contrasting and variegated foliage – copper beech, silver leaved maple, weeping limes, white poplars, silver holly, blue spruce and so forth.

Restoration at Waddesdon began with a tree survey. Those damaged irrevocably in the 1987 gale had to be removed and their stumps ground out, and in the appropriate places replaced by saplings. There had been no replanting since Ferdinand's original installation and con-

BELOW LEFT
The aviary at Waddesdon with a little visitor

BELOW
Ferdinand de Rothschild

sequently the great majority of trees were all approximately 100-120 years old. In some cases, such as the group of Austrian pines behind the aviary, they had reached maturity and had become a danger to the building. Regretfully it was decided to remove them – no simple task. This was achieved by attaching a chain suspended from a crane to the tree, the top half was then sawn off and lowered to the ground. The lower half of the trunk, weighing two tonnes, was then attached to the chain, sawn off at ground level and manoeuvred into a safe position for removal. The trunks were then collected by a lorry with a hydraulic arm that swung them from the ground to the back of the truck in one movement. The aviary was untouched!

The wooded area of the garden grounds provides the major part of the workload at present and much of it has had to be contracted out. A tree register has been compiled and replanting begun. A new woodland walk is planned, a box tree walk and an autumn glade.

The so-called daffodil valley is a wide, shallow sweep of grass on the side of the hill, between two wooded areas, falling gently downwards some 400 yards to the West Drive. It was planted with thousands of daffodils by James and Dorothy in memory of Alice. Owing to the ravages of a daffodil nematode, the bulbs have been greatly reduced and the valley is now to be sown with a wild flower mixture containing 60 species. This will add considerably to the naturally rich flora of the area. The various vetches included will especially attract blue butterflies and a good sized population should become installed in a few years time. (A board illustrating a few of the species present will be placed beside the path of the West Drive.) Some banks have also been sown with wild flowers, a modified "Farmer's Nightmare" mixture (*see p. 102*), and by careful management poppies were in bloom last year until October.

Alice's extensive rose garden is to be replanted this year but it will require various new varieties since, apart from losses through old age, many of the original cultivars have disappeared. Alice ordered her roses by the thousand, one invoice for 1,000 cutting briar stocks and 1,900 seed briar stocks suggests she also engaged in her own cultivations. Beth feeds her roses with bonemeal and good old-fashioned manure and sprays against mildew using a back-pack sprayer. Papers in the Waddesdon archives show that Alice ordered Joseph Bentley's "Selected English Bones", "degreased but retaining full fertilising value" and Bentley's Quassia and Nicotine Insecticide.

RIGHT
The rose pergola

A butterfly garden is to be included, adjoining the rose garden, and this is essentially a twentieth century innovation. Beth has realised that many of the new horticultural varieties of herbaceous plants have lost both their scent and their attractive nectar and a great effort will be made to obtain seed and plants of the more primitive "cottage garden" varieties. An excellent butterfly-luring Michaelmas daisy (renamed 'Butterfly') is available from Ashton. The original ice plant (*Sedum*) which used to attract scores of Small Tortoiseshells is not easy to find. For this purpose the new dark red varieties are useless and many of the pale pink ones have lost most of their charm for butterflies and bumble bees. It is proposed to experiment with a wide range of seeds of the pink types until one is found with the appropriate secretions. One

---

PROPOSED SUMMER BEDDING NUMBERS AT WADDESDON 1996

Terrace :	*Geranium* 'Alex' (red)	8,800
Shield Beds and Diamonds:	*Geranium* 'Aphrodite' – White	600
Red Lion steps: consider	*Heliotrope* 'Marine'	300
Conservatory:	*Geranium* 'Alex'	250
House Front (south):	*Geranium* 'Alex'	330
Vases (all):	*Geranium* 'Alex'	
or trailing geraniums		170
Additional Plants:		360
Blue Bands		
(including Shields and Diamonds):		
	Ageratum 'Blue Danube'	4,000
Aviary (Star bed):	*Begonia* 'Amy Jean Bard'	
	or White *Antherrinum*	900
30 Rings:	18 *Coleus* 'Midas'	540
	36 *Cineraria Maritima* 'Silver Dust'	1,080
Fountain beds – Outline :		
consider new scheme similar to old photos		1,300
Fountain beds – Centre:		
consider new scheme similar to old photos		4,300
North Avenue beds x 4:		
Stars:	Feverfew (4 x 525)	2,100
Triangles:	*Ageratum* 'Blue Horizon' (4 x 650)	2,700
Rings:	Yellow *Begonia* or alternative (4 x 525)	2,100

Scarlet geraniums in the Waddesdon parterres in summer.
The Vale of Aylesbury stretches beyond the trees

plant which attracts Red Admiral butterflies is *Ligularia*, but here again the latest cultivars will be avoided. Plum and pear trees are to be planted, as the fruit when ripe is very attractive to both Comma and Red Admiral butterflies. In the autumn there is nothing more delightful than to watch bright Commas flickering over purple plums lying beneath the tree, rising and falling in the sunshine. The backbone of any butterfly garden must be a series of buddleia; today early and late varieties are available, which extends their season, although the very dark purple cultivars do not attract the *Lepidoptera* they are irresistible – they are so beautiful.

The Dairy garden, with its own gardener, is a spring garden in the midst of restoration. In front of the building is a spread of conventional flower beds but elsewhere bulbs, and a fine collection of hellebores, are at present planted in agreeable confusion.

The lake on the far side of the Dairy was originally two concrete-bottomed ponds linked by a cascade. It is backed by a rockery constructed partly of artificial boulders (made from Portland cement by James Pulham) recently renovated in their original form. The adjacent banks have been planted with wild flowers and the perimeter of the lake itself with iris and rushes.

The Dairy has now become the work centre of the property. It is planned to give lectures, seminars and organise workshops as well as educational gardens for children. Although the National Trust are anxious to restore Waddesdon to its former Victorian glory, and to maintain the gardens to the high standards for which they were once famous, it is intended to introduce a variety of new and interesting features which will attract the public for a series of visits.

RIGHT
A plan of the proposed restoration at Waddesdon

FOLLOWING PAGES
LEFT AND RIGHT
The recently renovated rock garden

THE NORTH FOUNT[...]

Tree surgery and clearing have ma[...] restoration of the shrubberies aro[...] Fountain. Emphasis has been put on [...] all plants used were introduced befor[...]

THE CAR PARK

The land has been cleared and landscaped with a n[...] generation of trees, shrubs and ground cover. Ca[...] need no longer park in front of the Manor on t[...] North Avenue.

TAY BRIDGE

Tay Bridge has been cleared of overgrown shrubs and perennial weeds. A path has been made for public access. Planting will be carried out during the winter of 95/96.

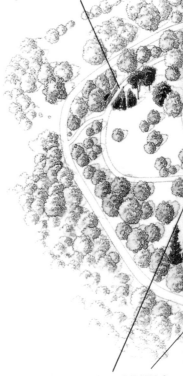

THE SITE OF THE ROSE GARDEN & BUTTERFLY GARDEN

Miss Alice's rose garden will be re-instated in 1996. Restoration will be based on photographic evidence. A butterfly garden will be created around the Aviary, a new feature for Waddesdon.

THE NORTH AVENUE

The circular beds have been re-instated with modern bedding schemes. Irrigation has been installed for the first time.

THE TULIP PATCH

Cleared of understorey vegetation in 1995. Tree surgery work has been carried out and underground maintenance begun. Pulham works have been discovered throughout the garden. Two goat grottos remain standing. This garden will be open in 1997 and will include a Children's area.

THE DAIRY, AND ROCK & WATER GARDEN

The Dairy building has been renovated and now serves as a working part of the estate, as well as for outside events. Academic lectures will take place at the Dairy. The Rock and Water Garden have been restored. The mechanism of the water feature has also been repaired.

EAST DRIVE

THE SHRUBBERIES AROUND THE MANOR

The borders around the Manor have been restored with plants used in Victorian horticulture. Hedges have been reinstated along with grass verges. Drainage has been renovated. Paths have been restored to original specification.

WEST DRIVE

THE PARTERRE

A new bedding scheme has been designed following the original pattern, and the beds mounded to the dimensions shown on Edwardian photographs. Yew hedges have been heavily pruned and the mechanism of the statues of the fountain repaired. The paths have been finished with hoggin surfaces and the drainage repaired.

DAFFODIL VALLEY

Late cutting of the meadow in 1994 has resulted in an explosion of wild flowers including orchids, primroses, cowslips as well as many species of butterflies and moths.

THE NEW ENTRANCE

Visitor flow was reversed in 1995, enabling the visitor to come into the property as originally intended. The Manor is now approached through open parkland grazed by sheep.

LIST OF GARDEN MACHINERY USED IN THE WADDESDON RESTORATION

The numerous minor hand tools and gadgets, protective clothing,
computers for tree inspection, artificial lighting etc are not included:

Large tractors with hydraulic loader

Powerful compact tractors

Hydraulically operated tipping trailers

Tirfor forestry winch and kevlar strops

Strimmers with vibration damping and electronic ignition

Lawnmowers with plastic bodies running on lead-free petrol

Light-weight back pack blowers (to collect fallen leaves)

Hand-held petrol vacuum for terrace

Hover attachment for loading leaves from piles on ground to trailer

Chainsaws

Electric hedge clippers

Portable electric drill (battery powered)

Small battery operated clippers for marjoram

Lap-top computers

Mole plough

Rotovator

JCB and compact equipment

Knapsack sprayers

Scaffolding tube used as bulb planter

Measuring wheel

Hydraulic platform for cutting hedge at box view

Auto-irrigation and Cameron dilutor for feeding

Architectural lighting below ground and on stage set type masts

Water bowser and pump

Rotary brush for tractor

Sabbo Roberine ride on mower (8 ft cut)

Reciprocating mower with other attachments for working on banks and confined spaces.

THREE

Exbury
by Lionel de Rothschild

"A banker by hobby but a gardener by profession" is one description of my grandfather Lionel de Rothschild, and few members of the family have been so single-minded in their devotion to gardening. Lionel had his own little garden at Ascott at the age of five; it soon became his passion.

Lionel's other childhood home, Gunnersbury, was the first major Rothschild garden in England, and one of the most famous in its day. It had a long history, from King Canute's niece to Edward III's mistress to George II's daughter. In the days of Lionel's grandfather, Baron Lionel, huge trees had been transplanted to Gunnersbury Park, "worthy companions" for its famous cedars. Also famous were the rose arches on the lawn – still there – and the astonishing variety of fruit, including a Pinery producing huge Providence pineapples weighing up to 15 pounds. A beautiful Orangery housed two enormous tree ferns (*Dicksonia antarctica*) sent by the Governor of Tasmania in 1873, each approaching 33 feet high, and weighing well over a ton.

In Leopold's day (Lionel's father) Gunnersbury fruit continued to be famous, especially their 1,200 fruit trees in pots, rotated in greenhouses to give the maximum variety and longest fruiting season. Roses also remained prominent, including a single bed of up to 600 'Caroline Testout' roses, and an observer in 1883 was delighted to see the graceful lawns "unmarred by set patterns of flower beds". It was in this period that the gardens developed a series of features, as at Ascott, Halton, and particularly Ile de France – a heath garden, an ivy garden, a bamboo garden with over 30 different species and varieties, an Italian (or Swiss) garden, an annual garden and, above all, a Japanese garden. The inspiration for

RIGHT
The Burmese Temple bell,
which originally hung at
Gunnersbury

this, especially the bamboo avenue, originally came from photographs taken by Lionel (an outstanding photographer) of a Japanese style garden on Lake Como, supplemented by photographs and paintings of gardens in Japan. Planted in 1901, this caused a sensation, stepping-stone paths winding through bamboos, palms, acers and aralias, past stone lanterns and over a slender bamboo bridge trailing white *Wisteria sinensis,* leading to an elegant Tea House. An astonished Imperial ambassador told Leopold, "Marvellous! We have nothing like it in Japan."

Leopold took hybridisation seriously at Gunnersbury, and is famous for his prize-winning waterlilies, having 50 different varieties on the pond, and fantastic tender blue ones in special heated tanks, notably the famous Australian *Nymphaea gigantea* 'Hudsoni'[a]. James Hudson, the gardener at Gunnersbury House, particularly inspired Lionel for, in spite of the many set-piece gardens within a garden, he was a keen proponent of exactly Lionel's sort of landscaping, detesting carpet bedding and ribbon borders. He wrote "Get rid once and for ever of all idea of formality and then try to imitate nature, or rather work in accord with nature." For Lionel at Exbury "the whole object of a garden [was] to beautify nature with colour". Although he took his cue from Gunnersbury and its gardeners, above all he was inspired to do something quite new, quite different, with rhododendrons.

The family had already shown an interest in rhododendrons, in a general way: Baron James at Ferrières, for example, was credited with having encouraged the introduction of these hybrids into France. In the first part of this century there was a flood of new species, chiefly from the Sino-Himalaya; with their immense range in variation of colour and size (few, if any *genus* can compare) it was small wonder that they appealed so singly to those two Rothschild genes, the collecting gene and the hybridising gene!

In 1912, after his marriage to Marie-Louise Beer, Lionel moved to Inchmery, on the shores of the Solent, adjoining the Exbury estate. He had already experimented with a handful of hybrids at Gunnersbury when young (the details are lost); now he was determined to try his hand on a grand scale, and the New Forest with its oak trees had the right acid soil. Lionel planned his house and his garden at Inchmery, a mixture of formal and informal. He even planned to move the road that ran behind the house further north but family lore has it that he was prevented from doing so because there was a postbox at the end of it.

ABOVE
Lionel de Rothschild feeding his tame robin, which flew to greet him as he entered the Home wood

In 1918 the opportunity came to buy the whole of Exbury. Lionel set about enlarging Exbury House in neo-Georgian style, cladding it in yellow stone and taking care not to damage a magnificent *Magnolia grandiflora* on its west face; perhaps he remembered Hudson, who had written "adjust the building … and save the tree." To the east he made a small Italian garden, lined with rose beds and herbaceous borders, with, in homage to Gunnersbury, two small lily ponds specially heated to grow the more tender varieties. But the main focus was the woods extending away from the house which were formerly prime pheasant cover. There were several fine cedars lining the entrance glade, some now gone, the saddest casualties of the great storms of 1987 and 1990, as well as a wonderful plane tree (*Platanus orientalis*), layered into a group of four sinuously serpentine bodies. My grandmother remembered that the first thing Lionel showed her, billhook in hand, as she stood bemused by the tangle before her, were the cypresses (*Cupressus sempervirens*). These had been planted from a cone from a wreath which had fallen from the Duke of Wellington's funeral *cortège* in 1852.

In 1918 four men began trenching the Home wood; in the autumn of 1919 work started in earnest, with 150 men double-digging the ground two spits deep, mixing in some peaty leaf mould from neighbouring woods but no manure or artificial fertiliser (of which Lionel disapproved). They did use spent hops, another trick learnt from Gunnersbury, and this is the abiding mnemonic smell of the gardens for one of the retired gardeners. They dug for ten years. They were followed by a team of 60 gardeners to do the planting; an additional 15 worked in the greenhouses. A further 200 men built new houses, a bothy and a club. Local materials, especially oak, were used throughout, worked by Lionel's own sawmill; the exception was the two acres of greenhouses, where finest imported teak was used but the 150 tons of steel fittings were fashioned by his own blacksmith.

A large Orchid House held an astonishing collection for which Lionel was to become almost as famous as for his rhododendrons; a tropical house held vireyas and other tropical flowers and fruit, but fruit did not play as big a part at Exbury as at Rothschild gardens of the previous century. Other glasshouses held collections of hippeastrums, clivias, amaryllis and nerines. Where, for example, Halton's 50 greenhouses were primarily given over to the entertainment of Alfred's guests, with his out-of-season fruit, complicated table-arrangements of orchids and 40,000 bedding plants, Lionel's were devoted to the single-minded pursuit of excellence in his own hybrids in whatever *genus* he chose. Pride of place went to the vast Rhododendron House, 100 feet by 50 feet, designed by the firm[b] who had built the one at the Royal Botanic Gardens, Edinburgh, but erected by his own men in 1926. It housed the tender rhododendrons and was later much used for forcing or retarding particular plants he wished to use as parents.

The soil may have been right but the rainfall was not. Lionel repeatedly complained that "the worst place of all for summer rain is ... Exbury". He sunk boreholes and built a large red brick water tower housing two 20,000 gallon tanks, and laid 22 miles of pipes, capable of delivering a quarter of a million gallons daily. These are still partially in use, now supplemented by another borehole, new reservoirs and plastic piping. Ten acres were planted the first year; eventually the gardens occupied some 200 acres, with 26 miles of paths. Whether Lionel intended to enlarge his garden still further is unclear; another war and his death intervened.

ABOVE
Tree ferns in the Orangery at Gunnersbury, 1873

RIGHT
The Tea House in the Japanese garden at Gunnersbury

The first part of the garden he developed was Home wood. At the entrance to the glade he hung the Burmese temple bell which had been at Gunnersbury (*see p. 19*); friends joked that it was used to summon him back to the house for dinner. As Home wood developed, he planted the scented *R. Loderi* from Leonardslee, a walk of *R. augustinii* which he repeatedly interbred to reinforce the bluest and hardiest selection, and some magnificent *Magnolia campbellii*. Here he also planted *Hamamelis mollis*, the first Latin name my mother taught me and the first I have taught my children.

St Mary's spring still bubbles out among giant *Gunnera manicata*, under the Japanese bridge and into the top pond, which is fringed with the Exbury range of deciduous azaleas and filled with huge lazy carp and golden orfe. On a little island in the pond there is a fine swamp cypress (*Taxodium distichum*) and a nesting place for a troop of ducks. Little rivulets, my favourite part of the garden, join the top and middle ponds; the lower pond reflects many older evergreen azaleas. Below the ponds the Camellia Walk takes one into the sheltered winter garden, the last area Lionel developed. Here stands a huge tree of the rare pink form of *Manglietia insignis*, from seed collected by Farrer; Lionel remembered his roots and also sent seed to Gunnersbury. Here too are the big-leaved rhododendrons, including *R. Fortune*, some with leaves over two feet long and vast trusses – a truly majestic sight. At the bottom runs the Beaulieu river, teeming with yachts and wildfowl.

The daffodil meadow links Home wood to Witcher's wood, where Lionel planted many hybrids, such as his early-flowering *R.* 'Avalanche'. Just opposite is one of the rarest trees in the garden, Farrer's spruce (*Picea farreri*) – also one of the scruffiest! A straight path, Lover's Lane, runs down the wood to Gilbury pier and parallel is the Lady Chamberlain Walk, displaying Lionel's fine *R. cinnabarinum* crosses with their waxy lapageria-like flowers. A small iris garden lies before the bridge linking Witcher's wood to Yard wood. Lionel had hoped to buy the land at the bottom of Gilbury Lane, which divided his garden at this point, but he could not; tiring of opening and closing the gates across the road, he built an elegant stone bridge here, though the cost

RIGHT
Exbury House in spring

LEFT
R. 'Naomi', named after Lionel's younger daughter

BELOW LEFT
The plane tree layered itself into fantastic contortions

RIGHT
Evergreen azaleas, Pieris formosa 'Wakehurst' and Gunnera manicata in front of the Japanese bridge in spring

Below
The middle pond, the heart of the garden

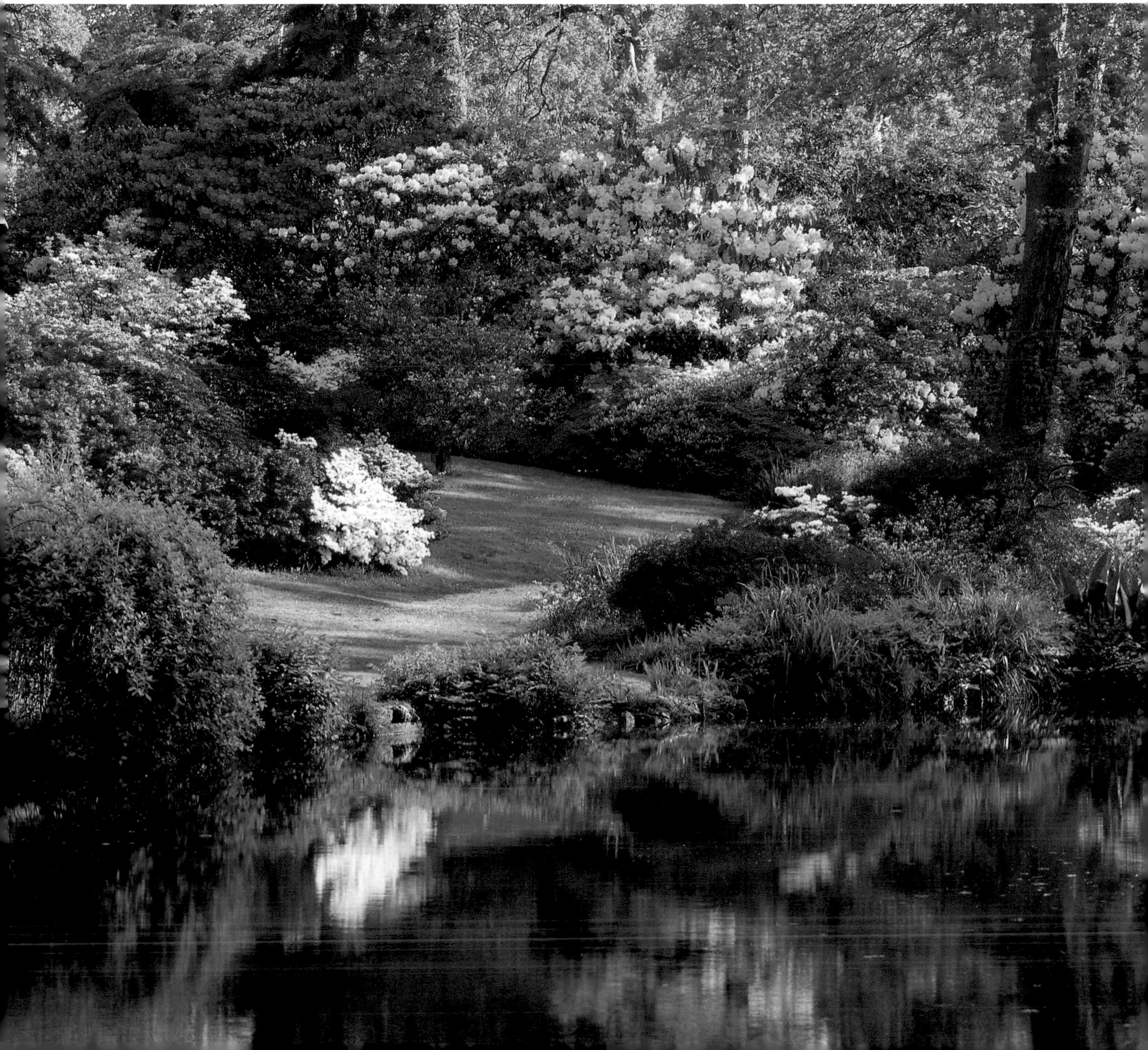

rather shocked him and he jokingly referred to it as "Lionel's Folly". He sited a pair of magnificent fastigiate beeches in front of the bridge, two towering *Magnolia campbellii* and a large planting of the pink *R*. Naomi, one of his earlier crosses and personal favourites; here nested some robins which he fed by hand.

The Azalea Drive goes down the hill; on its right is the two acre rock garden, completed in about 1930 in an old gravel pit. The sandstone rocks were brought from Wales and, as well as overhead sprays, Lionel installed pipes sunk behind the stones to enable water to be applied underground to plants growing in the crevices. Lionel wrote of his experience of growing alpine rhododendrons and admitted some failures - chiefly due to honey fungus and waterlogging – concluding wryly, "gardening would be too easy if it was always a success". He planted a fringe of rhododendrons with lighter foliage round the edge, mainly *R. yunnanense*, to set off the delicate alpines.

At the top of the Yard wood, with its many yews, is the Domesday yew, so old and hollow that we used to crawl inside it as children. The road curves back past Augustinii Corner, a typical Lionel planting in family colours of blue *R. augustinii* and yellow *R. campylocarpum* Elatum. Then the wood opens out into the summer garden with its own series of cascades feeding into Jubilee pond (George V's Jubilee of 1935).

Exbury garden was both planned and grew organically; Lionel was both collector and landscaper. He wrote: "The real art of gardening is to make a plant that has come from distant lands not only look at home but feel at home"; and "the real art of gardening is not only to group plants to make a picture but also to see that colours mingle well. What has been done in herbaceous borders can just as well be done on a large scale in the woodland with azaleas and rhododendrons."

A contemporary[c] compared Lionel to Philip Sassoon of Port Lympne, whose mother Aline was a Rothschild: "He was to woods what Philip Sassoon was to herbaceous borders. Both of them had unlimited money at their disposal, both also had most discerning eyes for colour and effect, and both were past masters in that most necessary of the arts of life, the art of anticipation… Both could feel by instinct

RIGHT
Evergreen azaleas, candelabra primulas and acers reflected in the lower pond

the effect of their designs." To achieve precisely the right tone, Sassoon once bought an entire spectrum of Cartier cigarette cases as a guide for his gardener. To achieve precisely the right effect, Lionel would move plants frequently, their "little walks", but he was rarely entirely satisfied so he would shuffle them about again. Most rhododendrons were easily moved, some even when flowering, and if they were too large, he had no compunction in using the axe.

As with the herbaceous border, some plants were for the front line, some for the back row. Lionel strove above all to prevent colour clashes, avoiding purple with red or pink, or "sealing-wax" red with crimson; magenta flowers had to be kept away from the purer colours, orange-salmon azaleas from any other rhododendron or azalea unless white – which was "always useful". Purple itself he placed on its own in the woodland or next to yellow. While Lionel considered evergreen azaleas formed a good foreground to rhododendrons in flower, he would only place deciduous azaleas against the dark green background of rhododendrons which flowered earlier or later. Some plants were grown solely for their "startling" foliage, and Lionel would pick off the flower buds that displeased him.

He published detailed notes on every rhododendron species in its "series": of one he wrote that it was "not worth growing except for the rhododendron maniac who wants to have one of every species - I have it at Exbury, but one plant is enough." Despite his huge collection, Lionel still found room to conduct the Rhododendron Association's Trials from 1930-38, and created a huge arboretum with a geometric network of paths to house every tree one could grow in the British Isles. The scale of the gardens at Exbury is extraordinary and yet, as the editor of *Country Life* wrote just after Lionel's death, "Despite its size it possesses a feeling of intimacy"[d]. This is one of its greatest achievements. Lionel is famously supposed to have addressed the City Horticultural Society with the words, "No garden, however small, should contain less than two acres of rough woodland" - he certainly wrote a similar remark. Regardless of the grand scale of Exbury, Lionel was not like the Rothschilds of the previous century, who were said to be "determined to astonish one another", like James of Ferrières telling Paxton to "Make me a Mentmore, only grander." Put quite simply, Lionel was a woodland gardener.

RIGHT
Azalea Drive

No detail was too small for his attention. Probably 90 per cent of his private correspondence concerned horticulture. He kept card index files on all the hybrids and species and specimen trees, noting their exact position and giving their flowering date each year, with planting and underplanting notes added – for example by *Magnolia stellata* he scrawled "An attractive picture is made by planting this shrub in a group growing beneath it thickly grape hyacinths (blue). The two flower together." Tours round the garden were planned with military precision: certain rhododendrons showed particularly well with the sun behind them. The massed plantings were another feature of the tours: Lionel placed great stands of the same rhododendron, making a grand statement and then, remembering Hudson's "variety is infinitely better than repetition", did not repeat it elsewhere in the garden. He particularly liked the walk to come round a corner and then open out into a surprise dramatic vista.

As time went by, so to some extent his taste changed, harder colours giving way to "softer hues" in his plantings. His own hybrids mirrored this change in taste, with pure yellow always a goal. Sadly he did not live to see the pure yellow he sought, as *R.* 'Crest' (*see p. 67*) only flowered in the early 1950s. The sheer numbers are staggering, accounting for some 25 per cent of inter-war rhododendron hybrids: he made 1,210 crosses, of which 462 were named and registered. One aim was for purer colours: he particularly eschewed magenta, the bluish tinge in red. A second aim was to prolong the season with earlier and later flowering rhododendrons, to have something flowering almost every month of the year. He also wished to improve the forms or the hardiness of species by repeatedly "breeding in". Certainly he gained more pleasure from seeing his own hybrids flower "than from any other form of gardening." He passed on all sorts of advice and observations, but of paramount importance was "the necessity of careful choice of parents, as the care and time spent in raising a good batch of seedlings or a bad batch are just the same". Lionel himself followed this careful choice to extremes,

ABOVE
*Constructing the rock garden,
completed in 1930*

RIGHT
The rock garden today

making long detours en route to Exbury, or despatching the chauffeur thousands of miles in search of the best possible parents.

Friends also sent him plants: in the case of my particular favourites, the exquisite bell-like *R. cinnabarinum* hybrids *R.* 'Lady Chamberlain' and *R.* 'Lady Rosebery', the forms of the pollen parent *R.* Royal Flush were sent by one of Lionel's gardening mentors, J.C. Williams of Caerhays. It is characteristic of the myths surrounding Lionel and his hybrids that one story has him seizing the trusses of *R.* Royal Flush from the vase at the end of the Rhododendron Show and motoring down to Exbury to make these crosses after dark!

Gifts went the other way too: following a weekend visit to Exbury, one young friend returned home to be rung by the station master with the words "A wagon load of rhododendrons has arrived here from Exbury for you!" The celebrated yellow hybrid *R.* 'Hawk' is said to have been the smallest seedling in a pan of which he gave all the rest away; when he made this cross a second time he achieved the best form, *R.* 'Crest'. Lionel did nearly all his hybridisation himself, by hand. He also helped fund many of the plant-hunters of the day, particularly Kingdon-Ward with his affinity for yellow.

Lionel's hybridisation was not limited to rhododendrons. He developed the famous Exbury range of deciduous azaleas, avoiding the "simile of the paint box" but mating pink with pink, white with white, yellow with yellow and so on. Many thousands of seedlings would be planted out, flowered, ruthlessly selected and then crossed again. It all fuelled the legend: as one admirer commented, "Exbury's nice sense of discrimination is proverbial: the contents of their bonfires would, in other hands, be a source of pride." He also hybridised other species, most notably nerines and orchids, and won innumerable prizes for his plants.

One year frost damaged the Chelsea Flower Show exhibit the day before opening: a quick telephone call and fifteen lorries of dug-up shrubs duly left Exbury at 4 o'clock in the morning to mount a "staggering" display. He was well served by his head gardeners, first Fred Kneller and then Arthur Bedford, who had been at Gunnersbury. But it was Lionel at the centre of it all, with his dominant personality, Lionel doing everything he set himself to do extremely well, with his unique knowledge and capacity for thoroughness. At Exbury lay his life's achievement.

ABOVE
The network of paths in the Arboretum, photographed by the Luftwaffe

Then came the Second World War. Fuel and food shortages meant many of the fabulous collection of orchids were let go to anybody who wanted them, and the greenhouses were given over to growing vegetables; an exception was made for the cymbidiums, which were considered by the Ministry of Agriculture to be of national importance. Lionel died in 1942 and the house was requisitioned by the Navy. Bombs straddled the park in front of the house and destroyed the Rhododendron House. Marie-Louise kept things going with the help of a skeleton staff. During her husband's life she may have felt, if not excluded then unequal to his knowledge; after his death she became quite an expert in her own right, sitting on the Rhododendron Committee of the R.H.S.

When my father, Edmund, returned from the war much had to be done. A more commercial *régime* was imposed and the wholesale nursery side developed. Inevitably things were lost, destroyed or even sold - statues that had come from Halton, plants from the garden and greenhouses if an order was short, even rocks from the rock garden. Tragically, the arboretum, which had survived the war, if a little overgrown, was now grubbed up for farmland. Luckily many beautiful and unusual specimen trees survive in the garden itself. Most important of all, the garden continued.

A new range of deciduous azaleas was developed, the Solent range which now lines Lover's lane. Edmund made some good new crosses but the single most important plant in post-war rhododendron lore is a species, *R. yakushimanum*. Lionel ordered two plants from the Japanese nurseryman Koichiro Wada in 1933 and another in 1938. When his wartime head gardener, Francis Hanger, left Exbury to become curator of Wisley he took a plant with him; at the time he described it as "a layer from the original introduction" though later versions have it as a separate plant. When exhibited in 1947 it was a sensation and won an instant F.C.C. With rose-pink buds opening white, soft brown indumentum like felt under green leaves, tolerance of cold and sun and above all a mound-like compact shape, this was and still remains the wonder rhododendron of the age. No rhododendron has been as much used for hybridising – a compact plant for everyman's garden. It is the single plant I invariably recommend to people who want "just one rhododendron."

No garden is static, and there have been changes. More evergreen azaleas have been planted, especially around the middle pond,

ABOVE
The pure yellow R. 'Crest'

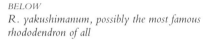
BELOW
R. yakushimanum, possibly the most famous rhododendron of all

making it very much a central feature – the Azalea Bowl. A river walk has been created at the bottom of the garden, leading to View Point. A new bog garden lies beside the rock garden, and the rock garden itself, the first thing to fall into disrepair, has been restored. New areas are also being developed round an enormous old beech tree in Yard wood. Within the framework of the garden every new generation leaves its mark. Where Lionel planted with a keen eye for colour and juxtaposition and liked the massed spectacle, my father tends for the kaleidoscopic effect. He has been ably assisted by some fine head gardeners, including Fred Wynniatt, Doug Betteridge and Paul Martin.

The drought of 1976 and the storms of 1987 and 1990 did some damage, but they also cleared new vistas. We have now appointed our first woman head gardener, Rachel Martin. My brother Nicholas has created an unusual and successful rose garden in memory ofmy mother, Elizabeth: in an area surrounded by yew hedges with a wisteria-covered gazebo and a sundial, where once Lionel had tulips, stands a pair of Tasmanian tree ferns, irises, paeonies, delphiniums, lupins and a multitude of standard roses, surrounded by an edging of lavender. I like to think of this as coming back full circle to the type of

RIGHT
A bank of white R. 'Palestrina' by the cascades in Yard wood

BELOW
The bog garden, one of the new developments

garden so loved by Leopold at Gunnersbury, combining roses and tree ferns. The greenhouses are now mainly used commercially. The rump of the cymbidiums went to a great friend of Edmund's and would have been returned to us in due course but sadly they all died. The nerines were sold in the early 1970s and many were bred on for twenty years[g] in a rigorous programme of which Lionel would have been proud; we recently acquired the collection, so they have come back.

The biggest change, of course, is the public: Lionel opened the gardens for occasional charity days, but it was not until 1955 that the gardens were properly opened to the public. Even then it was not all day every day: I remember my mother telling me that she was showing the then Russian ambassador round one Saturday morning and urged him to hurry with the words, "We must go now, Mr Ambassador, the public will be coming in a minute", only to meet the astonished response, "You open these beautiful gardens to the public?" The gardens, tended by eight full-time gardeners, are now owned by a family charitable Trust. They are open in their entirety for the Spring, Summer and Autumn. We have about 100,000 visitors a year.

Finally we have embarked on an ambitious plan to tag all the rhododendrons and specimen trees, except azaleas, with numbers and plot their details on a database. So far nearly 17,000 metal tags have been affixed, and innumerable bits of information entered on computer[h]. As some tags represent groups of plants we will probably end up with a count of some 25,000 plants, with a further 10-15,000 azaleas unaccounted for – probably one of the biggest projects of its kind ever undertaken. Lionel, "banker by hobby but gardener by profession", with his detailed card indexes, would have been proud, as I think he would have been of all Exbury today.

FOOTNOTES:
a) Later called 'Hudsoniana'   b) Mackenzie and Moncur Ltd   c) Viscount Templewood
d) G.C. Taylor, 1942   e) The late Sir John Carew Pole of Antony, Torpoint in Cornwall
f) Also Rock, Forrest, Farrer and Comber   g) By Sir Peter Smithers   h) By Michael and
Beverley Lear

RIGHT
Alliums mingle with roses around the sundial in the new rose garden

FOUR

Ascott

Ascott was originally a farmhouse built in 1606 by James I. When Leopold acquired it, together with 90 acres of land, from his uncle Mayer de Rothschild, it formed a portion of the Mentmore Estate in Buckinghamshire. In 1874 Leopold remodelled the house in Tudor style, incorporating the old farm building within the new. He employed the architect George Devey, to carry out the work. Leopold laid out the garden himself after discussions with Devey, but he depended far more on the advice and skill of Sir Harry Veitch*, whom he had known well in Gunnersbury days (*see pp. 48-50*).

It was possibly Sir Harry who was the admirer of Francis Bacon. Leopold's mother – who was an excellent gardener herself – was worried by her son's lack of erudition and wrote in her diary ".... he knows nothing and has a horror of books." Leopold was then five years old, so he may well have changed his views as time went on. Be that as it may, the Ascott plan closely followed Bacon's design for an "ideal garden"[1]. He had suggested that 30 acres was about the right size, to be divided into four acres of lawn in the front of the house, 12 acres of main garden in the centre and a wilderness of six acres at the perimeter. In the main garden, Bacon proposed borders, knots, espaliers, bowers and well grown trees. Tucked away beyond this was to be a herb garden and an orchard. These dimensions and instructions were followed at Ascott, although it lacked a knot garden. A writer in the contemporary *Gardeners Chronicle* drew attention to the unusual contrast of the formal *parterres* and topiary with the natural scenery of the wilderness and the distant views of the Vale. "What makes Ascott unique ... is the way in which these contrasting styles are associated."[2] Perhaps he missed the Tudor model.

RIGHT
Formal planting at Ascott

Francis Bacon recommended fountains in his "Prince-like" garden "for fountains they are a great beauty and refreshment". Leopold installed several at Ascott, two of which were designed by a fashionable American sculptor, William Wetmore Storey. He did not follow Bacon's counsel to avoid "unwholesome" pools and his lily pond and water garden, even if they attracted the flies and frogs to which Bacon objected, added great charm to the formal design of the surroundings.

Leopold was essentially a horticulturalist; his taste in flowers was topical, and he greatly enjoyed them *en masse*. His Carnation House (designed by Foster and Pearson who also built the Ashton glasshouses) was 18 feet wide and it was not unusual for it to contain 500 Malmaison carnations all in full bloom He won a gold medal for these plants. His 1,500 'Miss Joliffe', a pink, clove-scented perpetual carnation, yielded about 50,000 flowers annually. One visitor was staggered to see 1,000 scarlet nerines in one block of colour.

The garden was divided into different sections: Dutch garden, cottage garden, Jubilee garden, Golden garden, fern garden, rock and bog garden, alpine garden, a long tunnel of climbing rose and clematis-covered arches, and Leopold's famous herbaceous Madeira Walk. In the spring, a sea of forget-me-nots and daffodils spread out round the trees, thousands more daffodils were naturalised in the long grass towards the wilderness.

The topiary was remarkable, including a sundial, an outstanding work of yew-and-box art. The Roman numerals marking the hours were grown in box and the time of day was marked by the shadow of the tall central yew edifice. Round the perimeter was a box-trimmed motto: "Light and shade by turn but love always".

Leopold, since he was a London banker and for a long period also owned Gunnersbury, did not live continuously at Ascott. He gave his excellent gardener J. Jennings 80 gardeners to work with him and took a fatherly interest in them all. Leopold was a man of ideas and organisation rather than a practical plantsman. I doubt that he ever had

time to handle a spade or prune one of his innumerable bush apples, or could recognise crown rot, or even apple scab, but he was a joyful gardener and took almost childish delight in his wonderful flowers, which were bigger and brighter and more scented and more perfect than anyone else's. He loved to see them win medals at the R.H.S. shows! Professional botanists scoffed privately at this attitude and Sir Edward Salisbury remarked sarcastically that a begonia the size of a soup plate was the exhibitors' ultimate ambition. But the art of horticulture is not botany. Like many Rothschilds, Leopold had a superb memory, drive and energy, and paid attention to detail, which ensured the success of an agreeable hobby on a large scale.

The vegetable garden and orchard – tucked away as Bacon had advised 300 years previously – each covered ten acres. One unusually interesting collection of variegated plants filled the Golden garden – golden yew hedges (five feet high and four feet thick) golden holly, golden *Cupressus*, variegated privet, golden *Thuja*, but most marvellous of all, the enormous golden cedar. There were many fine trees at Ascott, quite apart from the inevitable blue spruce; two wonderful Japanese maples, 15 feet tall, blazed away in the Autumn, and there were copper and cut-leaved beeches, huge oaks and elms, paper birch, various weeping willows, magnolias and an Iron tree, 12 yards in diameter.

The house at Ascott was encased in creepers and climbers. They were even trained carefully round each chimney stack and window frame. Perhaps the most impressive plant in the whole garden was the enormous wisteria growing against the front elevation. It was the absolute epitome of floral glory. Another generation at Ascott was persuaded it was destroying the brickwork and menacing the very foundations of the house, and reluctantly cut it down. Faced with this gloomy prospect, I myself would have underpinned the wall, repointed the tiles and waited!

One of the trickiest and most important aspects of a large garden is its relationship with the house in which the owner lives. For instance, it is necessary to be able to walk out onto the terrace easily without pausing to negotiate steps. If there are flagstones, they should be narrow – not like a landing strip for aircraft. There must be a lawn but also trees to soften the glare and break the breeze. The flowers near the house must be neither suburban nor ostentatious. Ascott achieved this more successfully than any other Rothschild dwelling

ABOVE
Marie Perugia, a very good gardener

RIGHT
Leopold de Rothschild in his garden at Gunnersbury

BELOW
A corner of the garden at Ascott

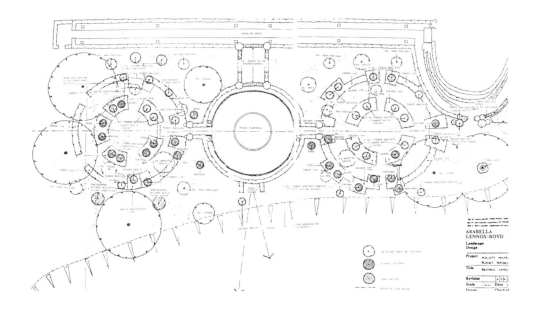

ARABELLA
LENNOX-BOYD

LEFT
Plan of the Zodiac garden at Ascott

BELOW
*Sign of the Zodiac: The frame of Pluto to
be covered by box*

and the endless stream of visitors always enjoyed themselves hugely, sitting and talking on the terrace.

Anthony de Rothschild (Leopold and Marie's son) gave Ascott, with an endowment, to the National Trust to ensure its survival, but continued to live there. The Trust would have liked to have kept the garden inviolate as an example of Victorian landscaping and horticulture. However, Anthony and his wife, and today his son and daughter-in-law, quite rightly are inclined to add to the garden themselves. The planet, or zodiac, topiary which Evelyn and Victoria have designed is imaginative and attractive – a twentieth century inspiration. All the planets and their moons are shown by well-executed symbols clipped out in box and their juxtaposition indicates the owners' birthdays.

The National Trust considers that such a *régime* is dubious since it must result in a steady erosion of the garden's original character. In one sense this is true, but if the owner and creator has left the scene you cannot immobilise a garden, like a work of art in a museum. It then becomes dull and loses its spirit, even if the box sundial – now clipped with machinery – would continue, obediently, to mark the hours. Come what may a garden must continue to grow.

FOOTNOTE
* *Sir Harry James Veitch (1840-1924), a leading horticulturalist of the day*

BELOW
A Magnolia near the house at Ascott

FIVE

Ashton Wold

My father Charles Rothschild (1877–1923, the first Lord Rothschild's second son) discovered Ashton quite by accident when he was in his early twenties. Whilst on a butterfly collecting expedition with the vicar of Polebrooke, he was impressed and charmed by the rich fauna and flora of the 500 acre woodland now known as Ashton Wold. Imagine his surprise when he found the property had been bought by his grandfather and left to his father, who was now a silent and uninterested owner.

Probably the principal reason why the site of the house, also known as Ashton Wold, and the fields surrounding it had escaped all development – not even a farm building had been erected there – was the scarcity of water in the area, which is 100 feet above the surrounding countryside. Charles decided he would like to make his home at Ashton and his father, Natty, readily agreed and built him the house on the plateau which was the highest point of the property. He erected a water tower and pumped water from the River Nene and the wells near Ashton village, two miles distant, to his house, and its garden, farms and cottages. The architect, William Huckvale, was a Tring man who employed local labour to build the house on the edge of the Wold. Natty also built a copious stable and garage, a steward's house, three lodges, a gardener's house with a bothy for his staff, two woodsmen's cottages, a home farm with a blue-tiled dairy and a dairymaid's cottage. It is a mini-disaster for Ashton that all the plans of the estate, including the maps showing the water supply and underground electric cables, were destroyed at Tring during the Second World War.

RIGHT
Wisteria and clematis mingle with an enthusiastic jumble of other climbers around a bedroom window

Charles Rothschild was an idealist and conservationist. He rebuilt the village of Ashton which was essentially in ruins, retaining six of the farmhouses to which he added large gardens. Only three cottages (dated 1607) were left untouched, including their traditional Collyweston tiled roofs. He provided the village with running, filtered water (until then the inhabitants had depended on wells), and constructed a bucolic drive from the village to Ashton Wold, two miles distant. My father believed that every cottage should have a bathroom and a large garden, in which he planted lilac, laburnum, a cherry and apple tree, and a stag's horn.

BELOW
A laburnum tree was planted in each of the cottage gardens by Charles

RIGHT
The Edwardian terraces at Ashton before they
were planted with trees and wild flowers
(the author with camera)

LEFT
The water garden about 1906

Charles gave prizes for the best garden and organised a grand annual flower show on the lawn at Ashton Wold, with a brass band and free champagne. The local newspaper remarked that 5,000 visitors turned up. Charles' shepherd, Fred Hill, always gained the most awards. Hill won over 2,000 prizes altogether at local flower shows; his cottage garden at East Lodge was perfection.

At the entrance to the courtyard at Ashton Wold the building faced south-west, with fields falling away towards Polebrooke and the lake, concealed behind the distant trees about half a mile from the house. This provided a natural terraced garden, the only three-tiered terraced garden among the Rothschild properties. 400 yards of flat-topped stone walls were erected (the stone was quarried locally) round the house, and another 200 by 100 yards of wall, ten feet high, formed the enclosed quadrangular kitchen garden, one side of which encompassed a series of greenhouses. Apart from the kitchen garden and the grounds dividing the house from the wood and the open fields, there were several discrete walled gardens including the rose garden with a stone sundial and paved paths, and a water garden with a sunken central pool encircled by flowers – roses, iris, catmint and a great variety of other cultivated and wild species. The water garden was typically Edwardian, particularly the arches of 'Hiawatha' roses separating it from the rock garden, and the stone steps with wooden seats, hooded in a canopy of 'Dorothy Perkins' pink roses, miraculously free from mildew.

In the centre of the rock garden was a thatched dovecote with a flock of white fantails, reached by stepping stones across a pond with fountains (rarely, if ever, playing), and a waterfall surrounded by rushes, iris, kingcups, Mimulus, and other marsh-loving plants. Small separate ponds were situated in each corner, backed with rocks. This was essentially Charles' garden where gentians and almost black, wild tiger lilies grew among the rocks, and near the apex of the rock piles were Austrian and Hungarian wild briars – a brighter orange than anything we can find today.

On the south side of the house a series of Edwardian flowerbeds were planted with conventional bedding-out plants, each bed rimmed with pale mauve violas. A grass enclave was surrounded by huge deodars and blue spruce, an incongruous legacy from Tring which looked stunning after a fall of snow but otherwise grated. In the terraced walls were small cavitities filled with soil and planted with a great variety of flowering alpines and some of the more familiar garden plants,

ABOVE
Charles Rothschild – botanist rather than gardener

BELOW
Rozsika Wertheimstein, a creative gardener with a special love of tea roses

campanula, aubrieta and *Dianthus*. Round the lawn at the bottom of the terraces was a necklace – 200 yards long – of herbaceous borders. One visitor to Ashton exclaimed, "It's like a beautiful cup in a beautiful saucer" and, although this remark annoyed Rozsika, my mother, it expressed rather well the agreeable, balanced design of the house and its terraces.

In his early twenties Charles was still influenced by the grandeur and luxury of the Tring hothouses and at Ashton began by engaging 14 gardeners, with a head gardener who was trained at Tring, and his son Charles Wright. Among the men was an orchid specialist who looked after his collection in a specially designed greenhouse. There was a collection of 2,000 orchids at Tring; from this Charles selected some of the rarer species to take to Ashton, adding to them as time went on. These included several of the early Tring crosses between *Laelia anceps* and *Cattleya*. Even as late as 1900-1910, the cultivation of orchids was at a relatively early stage and the pure white *Cattleya* which Charles gave to his father for his 70th birthday was considered a miracle. Today, white *Cattleya* are commonplace.

Charles brought back plants and seeds of the blue waterlily *Nymphaea caerulea* from one of his collecting expeditions around the world, and built a special greenhouse for them which contained two tanks each seven yards long by two yards wide, joined anteriorily and filled with rainwater collected from the roofs of the potting sheds. The sides of this house were completely covered with green ferns and a mat of other plants so that sunlight came only through the glass roof. The waterlilies' flowers were of a fantastic size and hardiness, and 60 years later, they were still as vigorous as ever. No artificial heat was necessary until the winter when the tanks were protected from frost, the water emptied and the corms treated with a light covering of farm manure. These flowers received an R.H.S. award in about 1900, and when they were shown again in 1940 they were still of a unique size and quality.

Behind the deodars, Charles planted *Ligularia* to attract butterflies and Rozsika built up a large collection of dahlias which filled the enclave. As a child, I loved the old 'Bishop of Llandaff' (a variety now lost) not only for its red and white striped petals and bronzed foliage, but because its seeds produced such an amazing crop of different coloured offspring. As for the scores of Red Admiral butterflies attracted to my father's *Ligularia* – that was never to be forgotten.

The kitchen garden was most attractive. The soil was brought from the Bournemouth area by train, to replace the calcareous boulder clay of the Wold. Down both sides of the gravel paths were wide herbaceous borders, planted with a collection of old-fashioned cottage-garden flowers, such as red hot pokers, paeonies, moss roses, Michaelmas daisies and Madonna lilies. The paths formed a cross with a sundial at the centre. The borders were flanked by cordons of fruit trees – different varieties of apples and pears – behind which lay rows of vegetables, strawberries and several raised asparagus beds. Greengages, apricots, plums, pears, cherries and figs were trained along the inside of the stone walls: On the outside were Morello cherries and 150 yards of peaches and nectarines enclosed in a glass and wooden frame ten feet high. Alongside this range was a double row, 200 yards in length, of hybrid tea roses, kept for cutting. These in turn were flanked with another cordon of apples and pears, and an orchard, part of which was caged against birds, growing gooseberries, currants, blackberries and dewberries.

One of the greenhouses was reserved for black grapes, another for green, while the large centre portion housed Charles' collection of cacti, some of which were 20 feet tall. I loved the cacti and, aged

OPPOSITE
Crabapple 'Golden Hornet' on the terrace at Ashton

ABOVE
Cherry tree in winter

BELOW
Frosted hogweed

seven, began a collection myself in a tiny, miniature model greenhouse, and missed becoming a cactus specialist by a bee's whisker! Alongside the greenhouses a sheltered bed was divided up into neat squares with Victorian twists, each square containing a species of wild iris, about which my father was an acknowledged expert. In 1923 he bequeathed the collection of rareties to my mother, but various botanical gardens such as Kew, Cambridge, Edinburgh, Oxford and Glasnevin, were permitted to select from them; Kew took 350 orchids which included seven species of *Vanda*, 15 species of *Cattleya*, 23 species of *Dendrobium* and a majority of the iris.[*]

After Charles' death in 1923, the number of Ashton gardeners was reduced to eight and the beds in front of the house were planted with roses, rather than annuals. The orchids, decimated by the species bequeathed to Kew, no longer required a specialist to look after them. Until the outbreak of war and Rozsika's death in 1940, the gardens at Ashton, in a somewhat lower key, remained beautiful and peaceful, set in a remarkably unspoilt landscape and still providing delicious fruit and vegetables.

But the end of the phoney war marked the end of Rozsika's garden. I moved to a cottage in the village, the house was taken over by the Red Cross, and the Helminthological collection from the Natural History Museum stored in the cellars. The Ordnance Corps was billeted in the stables and steward's house. During the five years which ensued, the herbaceous borders and flower beds at Ashton Wold became grassed over and the pergolas collapsed and disappeared. The terrace walls were pillaged and the saxifrage and other alpines gouged out from between the stones (I once met a man carrying off a sackful of these plants). The tool and potting sheds were ransacked, even the leather boots worn by the pony which pulled the mowing machine were stolen. The fire-fighting equipment, hoses, protective clothing and brass fittings vanished. So did the shotguns from the gunroom and the saddles and bridles from the locked stable store. The

PREVIOUS PAGES
The avenue at Ashton in winter

RIGHT
A winter view of the Ashton garden and fields beyond from a bedroom window

swans on the lake were shot. No invading army could have achieved more wanton destruction.

During the war years circumstances changed me from a lover of flowers and an appreciative onlooker – taking it all for granted – into a practical gardener. Furthermore, I was now 34 years old, and approaching the moment when a metamorphosis occurs and one emerges a middle-aged pruner-of-roses, a "sticker"-of-sweetpeas and a planter of broad beans. That moment was still to come.

At first I made a vain effort to save some of the rarer plants in the rock garden. I bicycled up from the village on my way to the cow-sheds, and weeded and watered. It was possible, while I was waiting to be called-up. During this hiatus I learned how to grow vegetables the hard way. I also discovered how beautiful asparagus ferns are when they are spangled with scarlet berries. Sometimes, trying to keep pace with weeds and cope with nagging war worry, I worked at night if there was a bright moon.

An extraordinary incident occurred when I was attempting to grow strawberries. A bale of straw was opened for spreading round the flowering plants. Out dropped a gold chain bracelet which I had lost and searched for in vain in a stubble field 18 months previously. It must have grown up with the next crop of wheat and been harvested and baled in that season's straw.

Before the outbreak of hostilities, all scientists had been placed in Reserved Occupation and were not allowed to join the forces or undertake regular "war work". But my life in the garden and on the farm was suddenly interrupted when I was directed to the code-breaking organisation at Bletchley. The rare plants in the rock garden were now overwhelmed by invading grasses and disappeared. The only survivors in the Ashton gardens were the fruit trees, the blue waterlilies and a few orchids, looked after by a casualty of the first World War, and warmed with two ancient oil stoves. The vegetables behind my cottage were devoured by rabbits.

The day I left Ashton for Bletchley I sat in the water garden – watching an unconcerned kingfisher – profoundly depressed and melancholy. The Holocaust; the war; my parents' deaths; the end of the garden. Nothing seemed to matter any more. Then I began to think back over the past and wondered idly about my parents' relationship with their garden. My father had never had time to sit at ease under the giant ash tree and smoke his pipe. He was a workaholic, senior partner of Rothschilds, deeply involved in tropical medicine, in world-wide conservation, in botany, in entomology, in unlimited charitable organisations and public duties. He loved his plants, particularly the iris, but the garden as such? No, not really. He was a dyed-in-the-wool naturalist, not a horticulturist, and my mother's rose garden round the stone sundial, with the blue flax waving so gracefully between the paving stones, barely impinged on his consciousness.

Rozsika herself was an aesthetic gardener; a creative gardener of a well-planned picture garden with grass lawns and paths, cascades of roses, banks of flocks, fiery Virginia creepers and alleyways flanked with purple cherrypie – and with a special love of tea roses and the dead white 'Frau Karl Druschki'. She undoubtedly derived a great deal of pleasure and satisfaction from the remarkably successful management of her 200 yards of herbaceous borders, (one stretch of which contained only yellow flowers), the walls full of alpines, and the skill with which she and Charles Wright appeared to keep the water garden ablaze with flowers, apparently perpetually in full bloom. On the other hand, I do not believe her practical gardening went beyond dead-heading the roses – and the idea of my mother with a hoe or hose was laughable. I do not believe she loved *growing* plants, only the beautiful and perfect end product was desirable. Even the flower vases in the house were arranged impeccably by the head gardener and only very, very rarely did I see my mother filling one of the beautiful metal bowls with tea roses.

ABOVE
*Melons growing at Ashton after
World War Two*

As children we helped in picking strawberries, gooseberries and currants in the fruit cages – the silver undersides of the leaves of the dewberries were unforgettable – but I never saw my parents carry a basket of fruit, let alone cut a bunch of grapes off the vines. Did my mother know that Charles Wright washed the bloom off the grapes, and presumably any foreign particles, with a forcible mist-fine spray like a little gun? I doubted it.

As I watched and wondered gloomily, two baby moorhens, like bumble bees, frisked across the surface of the waterlily leaves and vanished. Yes, this really was the end of Rozsika's and Charles' garden.

When the war ended in 1945 my husband, George Lane, returned from a P.O.W. Camp. In a mood of buoyant euphoria – the blackout misery had ended and rose-coloured spectacles took its place – we decided to enjoy family life and, in addition, to try to recreate the farm and the garden at Ashton. The house required drastic repairs and alterations and did not become habitable for a decade, so we lived in a cottage in the village for the next ten years and I concentrated on the resuscitation of the kitchen garden at the Wold. Times had indeed changed and it was essential to initiate luxury horticulture with a strong commercial flavour. I donned a pair of riding breeches and bought a delivery van…

At that moment, miraculously, H.C. Stanton came to Ashton. He was a superb gardener with an insatiable, exuberant love of flower shows, especially those which included classes for fruit and vegetables. Stanton continually but discreetly absented himself from Ashton to visit and judge at the R.H.S. shows. I turned a blind eye to this dubious activity, nor did I object to his exhibiting our flowers, fruit and vegetables – winning gold medals all along the line – although I did not myself care for competitive horticulture. Stanton had such astonishingly green fingers and such an intuitive and knowledgeable skill with plants that I let him do more or less what he liked and enjoyed the results and learned a great deal. He also possessed a keen eye and, although there was then a complete dearth of garden surrounding the closed house at Ashton, he planted cherry trees alongside each flight of terrace steps. Today, I am still grateful for this streak of optimistic foresight, for long after Stanton has gone to heaven, the cherry trees – now giants – provide a matchless backcloth for the lawns on which I grow my wild flowers.

PREVIOUS PAGES
Early morning: Queen Anne's Lace soon takes over

RIGHT
On arrival, puzzled visitors remark "Surely no one can live here?"

LEFT
Long grass, studded with wild flowers, laps up to the library steps like a wave

ABOVE
The Hawthorn Lane leading to Ashton

RIGHT
In spring narcissi flower beneath blossoming cherry trees

In a remarkably short period after his arrival, the Ashton kitchen garden returned to its former glory. The greenhouses looked wonderful. True, botanical collections were missing but we grew an unimaginable variety of pelargoniums, orchids, lilies, wallflowers, gooseberries, bananas, pineapples, figs and grapes, beans and carrots. I discovered, unexpectedly, in my own greenhouse, the incomparable flavour and aroma of freshly-picked bananas and pineapples, grown and pampered by a skilled gardener.

Stanton soon coaxed the Morello cherries into espaliers along the outside of the walls where, in the spring, they provided an icy white bridal veil for the stonework. He also transformed the sprawling cordons of apples and pears into stout green walls which bore a red and yellow curtain of fruit in the autumn. These were already 50-year old trees but they flourished under his care. In early April the peach frame glowed with pink flowers and I loved to walk along the path down the inside and view them against a blue sky. Alas! Stanton's green fingers turned to black thumbs where commerce was concerned and, after eight most enjoyable years, we both agreed he should move on to a larger enterprise, where there was no need to worry about marketing his gold-medal produce - and, hopefully, with an oil well hidden somewhere in the garden!

About this time our lives changed, and for the following 25 years we lived in Oxfordshire: Ashton became a weekend cottage and summer holiday resort. By the time we returned in the seventies to the Wold (minus its top floor), my taste in gardening had undergone a complete and drastic metamorphosis. I had become a wild flower and grass gardener.

The house at Ashton Wold became covered in a carefully thought-out jumble of climbing and adhesive plants – roses, wild and cultivated, mixed with quince, lilac, plum trees, ivy, Virginia creeper, clematis, buddleia (15 feet tall which brought butterflies round the bedroom windows), broom, wisteria, old man's beard, laurel, cherry trees and laburnum. Various birds, from woodpigeons to goldcrests, fly-catchers and blackbirds, mice and an occasional rat, shared the ivy with me. When visitors eventually found their way up the farm track (called a road) to the courtyard, they looked round uneasily at the creepers clambering over the roof and said, "Surely no one can *live* here?" In fact, I had discovered more or less by accident that plants like buddleia and lilac, and even broom, grow to a considerable height

OPPOSITE
The "Farmer's Nightmare" mixture of arable weeds

ABOVE
"Farmer's Nightmare" is excellent as cut flowers

planted against a wall and, while reaching for the sun, hide the architectural structure from view. During the war, when I lived at the cottage, I had become conscious of the flowers of tall trees – oak, ash and Norway maple. By chance I had discovered a wren's nest built entirely of flowers of a Turkey oak and that had delighted me and opened my eyes. Now I allowed the limes, *Philadelphus*, laburnums and lilacs planted by my father to grow into tall trees where they lost their hint of suburban decoration.

In days gone by it was only the outermost terrace wall that dropped steeply into the hayfields, but now the long grass lapped up to the library steps like a green wave. We lived in the fields, but they were well spangled with wild flowers, and, thanks to Stanton, cherry trees and other flowering fruit trees broke up the line of the terracing. The hothouses all became cold-houses, growing the true oxlip, hairy violet, Cheddar pinks, harebells and *Primula scotica* in pots and trays. One of the smaller greenhouses was kept for breeding butterflies. I still

BELOW
*Cowslips in the kitchen garden, grown in
rows like radishes*

cannot resist growing the climbing 'Etoile de Hollande' and 'Cedric Morris' up the back wall of the long greenhouse (May roses are too seductive), wild honeysuckle and white jasmine mixed in with them.

In the grass area immediately surrounding the house, I planted dwarf narcissi, tulip species, beargrass, lilies and iris, *Alliums* and a variety of bulbs that can compete with grass without "clashing" with the wild flowers – the seeds of which I had collected on local derelict airfields. Altogether, I now have about 120 native wild species – from wild garlic to bee orchids – growing in the lawns round the house, but I have no objection to uncultivated species *from abroad*, like bear grass and martagon lilies mixing with them. The gravel paths are lined with idle weeds – poppies, cornflowers, corncockles, feverfew, marigolds and flax – a mixture I have named "Farmer's Nightmare". These have to be resown every year. The rest of the grass area is mown only in September, except for a strip near the steps in front of the house, where we sit and gossip and drink tea.

BELOW
*Oxlips, cowslips, primroses and lady's smock
in the dining-room window,
awaiting transplanting*

The Ashton garden has come to symbolise the new sympathy with wildlife. The battle with weeds, the conquest of Nature, is a thing of the past. Nor is the garden a quiet Edwardian refuge from both the metropolis and the wilderness. It is John Clare's countryside resurrected. The compost heap behind the rose border contains recently hatched eggs of many young grass snakes and it is not unusual to see four adults abreast, swimming across the lily pond. Walking through the long grass which now covers the old tennis courts disturbs flights of blue and copper butterflies, rising like bright chips of metal seen against the sun. The redevelopment of a natural habitat has attracted various wild elements in from the cold. No less than four species of orchid have appeared in the ex-lawns, and in the group of trees and bushes in the centre of the courtyard, a nightingale breaks the silence on warm, dark evenings.

One fine afternoon in May, David and Valerie Scott paid me a visit. The crab apples were in full bloom, a snow-white clematis was clambering over a bronze-leaved *Prunus* and the grass banks were at their best; blue bells, cowslips, *Fritillaria*, white anemones, baby mauve and yellow tulips were all blooming together in glorious confusion – a Botticelli carpet. Next day I received a letter from David, who was at 95, certainly the most distinguished and gifted gardener of his day. It read, "Yours is unquestionably the prettiest spring garden I have ever seen". I framed that letter. I had been crowned!

Many people have asked me what event or experience turned me into a wild flower and grass gardener. I generally reply that one day the penny dropped and I realized with dismay that wild flowers had been drained, bulldozed, weed-killered and fertilised out of the fields and that we were now in a countryside reminiscent of a snooker table, and must do something about it. This has an element of truth in it but really I think I had merely returned to a nostalgic but genuine delight in wild flowers, in ridge-and-furrow lacquered with buttercups, quaking grass and the scent of new mown hay, and

"To see the meadows so divinely lye

Beneath the quiet of the evening sky."[1]

Nevertheless, there remains the ghost of my mother's roses at Ashton. A solitary plant of 'Irish Fireflame', a delightful single rose, although 90 years old, still flowers calmly alongside the kitchen garden wall, and an unnamed, wanton white rambler breaks down a new fence with an annual crush of flowers.

How long will they survive? How soon will the creepers be ruthlessly trimmed? When will the lawns be returned to tennis courts? The future of any garden is uncertain and mysterious, and flowers, wild or cultivated, like Shelley's dome of many coloured glass, will merely "stain the white radiance of Eternity"[2].

POSTSCRIPT

The wild flower gardening at Ashton has involved 20 years of experiment – trial and error. Today's procedure is as follows: we harvest the seed with a combine harvester from a hay meadow containing 119 species of wild plants, 70 per cent broadleaved, 30 per cent native grasses. We pass the harvested seed through a Boby dresser and drill it, in late September or the following March, into an appropriate seed bed with a John Hunter Rotary Strip Seeder. The stalks are dried and baled for hay. Sowing rate is 4 kilos to the acre if drilled into a close-cut sward and 8-9 kilos if drilled into bare soil. Slug pellets can, with advantage, be sprinkled behind the drill. If sowing a large area it should be grazed with sheep from October to Christmas the first year, and thereafter from August to Christmas.

To grow wild flowers near the house the same procedure can be followed, but more attractive results are obtained the first year if cowslips, primroses, violets and oxeye daises are introduced as seedlings (with a dibber). These can previously be grown in the kitchen garden like radishes in long single rows, before transplanting. Rotary strip seeding should be done parallel to the house, if close to the building.

Annual (arable) flowers such as poppies, corncockles, cornflowers and marigolds should be sown on a bare seed bed and then just covered with soil. Bird scarers are desirable until the plants have appeared above ground.

At present there are 150 acres of flowering hay meadows at Ashton - an extension of the garden itself.

FOOTNOTE:
* *The author donated Charles Rothschild's collection of pressed irises (38 species and sub-species – 159 specimens) to the Royal Botanic Gardens, Kew*

SIX

Ramat Hanadiv

The first garden planted in Israel by a member of the Rothschild family was a gift from Adelheid, the wife of Baron Edmond de Rothschild. In 1912 she created a memorial, now a public garden in Safed. 42 years later she herself was buried with her husband at Ramat Hanadiv (the Heights of the Benefactor). The seven acres of memorial garden which surrounds their tomb was planned by their youngest son, James. It is situated in a 1,000 acre estate, an area of no agricultural value as the soil is poor, but wonderfully suitable for the local flora.

The first occasion on which I visited Ramat Hanadiv was in April 1957, and I was overwhelmed by the sheer beauty of sheets of wild flowers, ranging from gladioli to orchids growing in improbable profusion in the area immediately surrounding the garden. It was possible to rest on a grass mound and count over 120 different species growing nearby.

Edmond had left instructions in his Will that he was to be buried in "the rocks of Israel". This wish was granted in 1954. After the State funeral, a man from each of the early settlements Edmond had founded in Israel – marching in order of their foundation – brought a sack of earth to Ramat Hanadiv with which to fill his grave. Nahum Sokolow eulogised his memory: "The Jew who works in the fields and on the plantations, in the vineyards and the groves, provides a living memorial to the Baron."[1] The tomb itself – buried in the rock – and the walls and paved areas were designed by the architect Uriel Schiller. Near the entrance of the garden is an engraved stone map showing the location of all Edmond's original agricultural settlements in Israel. Because of the great respect, almost reverence, in which his memory is held by Jewish people, this map

RIGHT
Wild flowers flourish on land adjacent to the Memorial Garden at Ramat Hanadiv

has proved of unfailing interest to many of the 250,000 annual visitors who come year after year to the garden.

James de Rothschild and his wife Dorothy selected the site for the tomb on account of its stunning situation, 150 metres above the surrounding countryside at the southern end of Mount Carmel, with a rocky centre to the plateau. They were delighted when I told them the garden was surrounded by a marvellous potential Nature Reserve, where the unique wild flora of Israel would add to the attraction of the Memorial, and in 1984 the surrounding area was scheduled as such. Edmond himself was a great gardener (*see p. 26*) who became interested in native plants towards the end of his life.

Schlomo Oren, a landscape architect from Kibbutz Yagur, planned and supervised the layout and planting of the area. The soil was brought from more fertile adjacent farmland and consisted of 30 centimetres of heavy clay spread over limestone. Water for irrigation, for the waterfall and the stone troughs in which waterlilies are grown,

BELOW LEFT
Baron Edmond de Rothschild

BELOW
Plan of Ramat Hanadiv

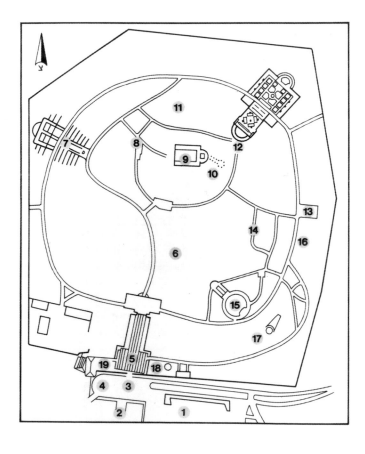

is pumped from the Zichron Ya'akov's municipal water supply. The garden is currently managed by a skilled and dedicated horticulturalist, Hugo Trago.

Originally, 78 species of trees were planted, which include six species of figs, six of palms and four species of pines and cedars. Among them, of course, is the eucalyptus tree, which Edmond introduced into Israel from Australia, and which he cultivated assiduously. These were used as shields for crops grown in sandy soil and exposed to destructive winds, as well as for draining swampy ground. Eucalyptus are seen in many parts of Israel today and are locally known as the Jew Trees[1]. Additionally, 90 species of flowering shrubs and 16 species of climbers were added at an early stage to the garden, most of which were obtained from Israeli nurseries, but some were imported from the South of France.

Paths now wind through the trees, flanked with flowers, ferns, succulents and ground-covering perennials, interrupted by grassy

BELOW
Sheets of local cyclamen cover the ground

enclaves full of wild flowers including various orchids, and sheets of local cyclamen. A beautiful feature of the garden is the gaps in the tall trees and the view over the wild country of the Nature Reserve and, in the distance, a strip of aquamarine sea.

Edmond, for the last decade of his life, was almost blind. Tragically his son James, following an accident when a golf ball smashed his eyeglass into his "good" eye, was left, too, almost sightless. This prompted him to install a fine garden for the blind at Hanadiv. The plants are various waist-high, aromatic herbs, labelled in braille in both Hebrew and English; in the background is the sound of running water.

On the southern perimeter, a large clearing is designed as a formal rose garden, with a stone wall and flagstones and classical arches. In the Mediterranean coastal climate of mild winters and hot summers roses flourish abundantly, so one looks across an improbable sea of pink blooms at a misty blue stretch of the distant hills of the Holy Land. It is wonderfully romantic.

Birds[2] are an essential attraction in a large garden, and the avian fauna of Israel is much richer than ours. 30 species are recorded breeding in Ramat Hanadiv, of which six are confined to the garden. They include glittering little sunbirds and the huge Eagle owl. Mountain gazelles[3] (an endangered species) are found in the Nature Reserve encircling the garden but these graceful, shy animals are too afraid of the noises of the cars and the voices of visitors to venture into the garden itself.

Edmond possessed what is perhaps the one outstanding quality of various members of the Rothschild family – the ability to be deeply and creatively interested in a variety of different subjects simultaneously. He was so interested in biological research that he founded the Institut de Biologie Physico-Chemique in Paris but, at the same time, continued to work on his fabulous collection of drawings and engravings which remains one of the finest examples of its kind, now in the Louvre in Paris. Yet Edmond spent most of his time and energy in his enterprise in Israel. His puzzled biographers described him as "encyclopaedically diversified rather than concentrated on one

RIGHT
Water runs right through the garden, an attractive and functional feature

consuming subject"[1]. Two areas just outside the perimeter of Ramat Hanadiv must be mentioned because they reflect two of Edmond's varied interests: horticulture and archaeology.

Immediately outside the garden the Archaeological department of the Hebrew University have excavated a Byzantine farmhouse and partly reconstructed the olive press, wine press and threshing floor – a most apposite addition to Edmond's memorial as it was he who promoted viticulture and the wine trade, and also the cultivation of olives in his original settlement in Israel. It is a sobering thought that by the turn of the century he had seen 200,000 vines planted to replace the original stock devastated by the *Phylloxera* aphid.

The second area on the perimeter of the garden which would have pleased Edmond is a demonstration terraced fruit and vegetable garden (a *boustan*) which would have supported one family. It illustrates the ancient Arabic methods of cultivation.

There is one urgent lesson to be learned from the now designated Nature Reserve, which also applies to some 40 reserves in the UK: scrub has encroached and has extinguished much of the wild flora I saw in the fifties when I first visited Ramat Hanadiv. It is essential to control scrub, preferably before it grows above six inches tall, even if additional funds have to be found for the purpose. The flowers should still reappear if stretches of ground are cleared forthwith, but it may soon be too late.

RIGHT
An improbable sea of pink roses in the foreground, leading to distant views of the Holy Land

Part Three

Past Gardeners

SEVEN

Beatrice Ephrussi – Villa Ile de France

Beatrice de Rothschild (1864-1934), Baroness Ephrussi, possessed the remorseless energy of her gifted uncle Edmond. She was beautiful, with white hair at the age of 20, creative and wilful. She had no children, and like her cousin Alice concentrated her interests and activities on her art collection and her gardens.

Few people can indulge their eccentricities but Beatrice was able to do so. She wished to create a beautiful setting for a museum in which to display her art collection, a blend of house and garden to make a single poetic unit amidst flowers and within the sound of the sea. She purchased a seven hectare rocky, narrow peninsula which jutted out into the Mediterranean like the prow of a ship; she flattened the top by means of dynamite and various quarrying techniques, installed elaborate irrigation, imported tons of fertile soil and created a plateau, on which she built the Villa Ile de France.

The Villa is a pink and white shell, lined with white marble, half Italian, half Spanish, encircled by trees in bloom and formal flower beds. It suited to perfection Beatrice's collection of *objets d' art*, pictures, tapestries and pink and green Sèvres china. Below the rocks lies the sapphire sea adorned with little white sailing boats – like butterflies darting between tree trunks – and behind is a background of misty hills.

It took Beatrice seven years of battling with 11 architects, plus builders, landscape designers, engineers, artists and 40 gardeners to create what she had envisaged. A touch of genius was the mini lake – a stone-bordered pool – in front of the Villa, reflecting it amid floating pink waterlilies. "I have achieved my purpose," she was supposed to have remarked, "by defying the laws of Nature and commonsense".

PREVIOUS PAGES
Beatrice's poetic unit – a pink and white shell lined with white marble

RIGHT
Looking into the Spanish garden at the Villa Ile de France

Beatrice entertained in the Ile de France but lived there only very sporadically. She bequeathed the Villa, with all her art collections, to the Académie des Beaux Arts[1]. Since her time the garden has no doubt undergone some drastic changes but she would be satisfied with the 100,000 annual visitors who appreciate her fantastic creation.

The Villa rests gracefully among palms, agaves, mimosa, almond trees, yuccas and citrus trees heavy with oranges. Calla lilies grow casually alongside flowering strelitzia and sprays of orchids. In the layout of the garden, Beatrice introduced many different styles – beginning with the Roman idea of a formal garden within a garden, then progressing through a Spanish garden, a Florentine garden, an exotic plant garden, a Japanese garden, a rose garden which contained a hundred different varieties, and a group of pine trees which once formed part of the English garden. There are fountains and a waterfall - an Oriental shawl of white water - and a Temple of Love perched above the French garden. The mixture is lighthearted – puff pastry – and even today embodies Beatrice's rather crazy *joie de vivre*. One of the garden's most enchanting moments is in spring when you suddenly come across a curving white balustrade, a flight of white steps cut into the rocks, and, across the tops of the flowering mimosa below, a view of the Bay of Beaulieu.

Some old invoices and inventories from 1911 give an idea of the profusion of flowers acquired each year – for instance 100 different varieties of English, French and Spanish carnations. There was a huge selection of climbing plants, plumbago, *Bougainvillea*, geraniums, casuarina, clematis and *Ficus*; roses were everywhere.

In front of the Villa, Beatrice placed two large vases from Tuscany, and in the garden are sculptured urns and several statues. At the turn of the century it was fashionable to introduce into corners, or peeping out of flowering bushes, elaborate sculptured fountains and marble statues, stone cornucopia and troughs decorated with carved heads – a link between art and the harsh outside world.

Succeeding generations have thought the Rothschild Victorian extravaganza – seen for example round the house at Halton – unsuitable in a garden, even ridiculous, but for a museum setting it was exactly right. The colour, the sunlight and the riotous flowers are all exciting, but this is not a garden where you are tempted to loll and daydream.

ABOVE
Beatrice de Rothschild, Baroness Ephrussi

RIGHT
A Temple of Love stands at the far end of the French garden

FOLLOWING PAGES
LEFT: View from the Florentine garden at the Villa Ile de France, looking out over the Mediterranean sea

RIGHT: A butterfly sits on the head of this winged figure in the Florentine garden

Like so many members of her family Beatrice had a restless desire for several different homes. Apart from the Ile de France, she lived in a villa in Monte Carlo, a large house in the Avenue Foch in Paris, a suite of rooms at Ferrières — her childhood home — and in the moated Château de Reux in Normandy. Beyond the ring of water, full of giant trout, the château was surrounded by undulating sward; the formal French garden with its *parterres* and topiary was hidden behind a screen of laurels. When Alix de Rothschild lived at Reux 20 years after Beatrice's death, for a time the grass was not mown and sheets of pale mauve lady's smock suddenly appeared — presumably propagating underground for half a century — alive with Orange-tip butterflies.

At Reux, Beatrice planted the most spectacular avenue of *Thujas* I have ever seen; two lines of gigantic trees were separated by a quarter of a mile stretch of icy cold water, their lower branches rippling the surface. A few white waterlilies and a pair of swans added a Beatrice touch to the scene. At Reux she certainly had green fingers where trees were concerned for her pear trees also grew to unbelievable heights, now standing some 50 feet tall.

I last saw her at Davos in Switzerland where, aged 70, she was dying of tuberculosis. She was still beautiful with a halo of snowy hair round her deathly pale face, and her piercing vivacity was totally unexpected in a bedridden invalid. Unfortunately on this occasion we did not discuss her garden.

ABOVE
A postcard sent 20 years ago shows the Thujas at Reux; in the distance is a piece of sculpture by Krike placed in position by Alix de Rothschild

LEFT
The exotic plant garden at the Villa Ile de France

EIGHT

Alfred de Rothschild –
Halton

At Halton, Alfred de Rothschild followed the fashion of the day and of his family, but he exaggerated joyfully. It is hard to say how much of his eccentricity and exhibitionism was spontaneous and how much was an act – a private joke – which somehow consoled him for the superior gifts and worldly success of his two brothers; one had been elevated to the peerage and the other had won the Derby! Did he enjoy caricaturing his family, all of whom were accused of emulating the British Aristocracy? He certainly enjoyed shocking his straightlaced sister-in-law, Emma, and even catered for a joke after his own death, for he bequeathed her a Greuze masterpiece – a saucy young woman with one bosom provocatively exposed, blowing a kiss to an unseen onlooker. My grandmother refused to have the picture in her home but Baron Maurice was delighted to hang it at Pregny.

Alfred built Halton in the style of a French château, and lit it by electricity. He bought beautiful Dutch and English pictures, Sèvres china and bejewelled snuff boxes; but he also gilded the woodwork, laid down marble floors, designed an outrageous Moorish smoking room, crammed the garden with marble statues, installed a circus ring, built seven different summer houses in the garden and, to provide for his weekend guests, employed five chefs and ten kitchen maids.

He also owned a private train which brought his friends to the nearest station, and directly motor cars were invented he acquired five for use at the château. A doctor was in residence in case a guest fell ill or had an accident skating on his rink. Alfred himself could never handle used coins, so freshly minted money was delivered every morning, straight from the bank.

RIGHT
Inside the Halton
conservatory

PREVIOUS PAGES
Halton with the conservatory

RIGHT
Alfred de Rothschild

BELOW
Alfred's astonishing floral basket

The interior of the house was arranged in enjoyable bad taste. Eustace Balfour, brother of the Prime Minister Arthur Balfour, a visitor from Aston Clinton, did not, for a moment, suspect a sly joke. "I have never seen anything so terribly ugly", he wrote, "Oh! but the hideousness of everything, the showiness, the sense of lavish wealth thrust up one's nose"... Was Alfred a naive exhibitionist or was he always smiling up his sweeping whiskers? We will never know.

When I was a child of seven, the family was taken over to Halton to have tea with Lord Kitchener. I was far more impressed by "Uncle Alfred" himself who, although 70 years old, gave us a spritely show in his circus. He acted as ringmaster, dressed in a black tailed coat and lavender suede gloves, and cracked a long white whip. Ponies obediently cantered round the ring, opened boxes, pulled out scarlet handkerchiefs and brought them to Alfred. He certainly knew how to astonish the guests! The ponies' headdresses and harnesses were decorated with coloured electric light bulbs. Some of the onlookers made sarcastic remarks but for me it was fairyland.

The Halton estate, a relatively small portion of the 30,000 acres bought in Buckinghamshire by Lionel de Rothschild, was bequeathed to his son Alfred, then aged 37. It was one of the most beautiful stretches of the Chiltern escarpment, lying between Tring and Aston Clinton.

The pseudo-French château was built (in 1882-3) with the assistance of an English architect, William Rogers. One of the most unusual features was the very large conservatory, with a domed roof, columns, arches and a flight of stone steps from outside, but also an entrance from within the house. The conservatory William Huckvale later attached to Ashton Wold (*see p. 169*) – although much simpler, without the dome – was vaguely reminiscent of the Halton edifice; at Ashton there were similar entrances from without and within. Alfred took an immense amount of trouble cramming his conservatory with palms, bamboos, a huge variety of ferns obtained from Veitch*, exotic flowers and roses at all seasons of the year. It was a completely theatrical arrangement, but impressive.

Alfred employed 50 gardeners and his terrain was ideal. It sloped down gently from the house and gave him the perfect setting for his beloved trees, which he planted full grown in groups of varying sizes. Each covert contained at least one specimen of every native British tree. He added various foreign species, carefully and cleverly selected for their contrasting foliage – from pale green to vivid scarlet – a fashion started by the family in France but widely imitated thereafter. Alfred was fortunate in finding magnificent Chiltern beech trees on the property and staggeringly beautiful views of the Vale and distant hills from every corner of the garden. One hot summer day, when white chalk pebbles began to show in the lawns, the gardener was told to paint them green; luckily it rained, and the grass grew quickly and hid the offending chalk!

The house was surrounded by conventional *parterres* and formal flower beds, carefully manicured lawns, winding paths and a surfeit of statues, urns, flower-filled marble containers, flights of steps and balustrades, fountains and rustic bridges. There was a corner called the Chinese water garden, then an Italian garden, a grotto and the lake. Alfred truly loved roses and he designed several rose gardens, the paths edged with marble and once again decorated with statues placed in rose-garlanded alcoves. He filled the *parterres* and formal flower beds with a fabulous variety of flowers.

The garden round the house was fenced off from the rest of the grounds which were, fortunately, not so well-manicured. Curiously enough Alfred could not resist building: he installed an elaborate Indian tent, an Austrian chalet, with bedrooms and a kitchen, a Pavilion of the Four Winds, a Temple Pavilion, a New Pavilion and a skittle alley (75 feet by 14 feet). In the kitchen garden he erected 50 glasshouses, where apart from orchids for the house and other tropical species, and fruit out of season, he grew 40,000 special bedding out plants, 10,000 carnation and 10,000 lily-of-the-valley in pots. The oft-quoted saying that in those days a man's status could be judged by the number of his bedding plants – "10,000 for a squire, 20,000 for a baronet, 30,000 for an Earl, and 50,000 for a Duke, but 60,000 at Waddesdon", was attributed to Field, Alfred's gardener.

Alfred loved birds and animals. He considered his peacocks essential as decoration in the grounds and he also specialised in various types of poultry, chickens, ducks and turkeys but insisted there should be "all stages present at the same time" – from eggs and day old chicks to cockerels in full breeding plumage.

In the garden, as well as in the circus ring, Alfred liked to astound his visitors. He had a large floral clock made, and a sundial bed, but the *pièce de resistance* was an enormous ten foot floral basket. It

NINE

Rothschild Parks

The first Rothschild park was bought by Amschel Mayer in 1816, situated in the Bockenheimerstrasse on the outskirts of Frankfurt (*see right*). It was apparently an extension of the garden but all we know is that it harboured deer cherished by the owner.

Although the Rothschild parks were recently described as "an indispensible supplement" of the châteaux[1], they have rarely attracted much public interest. Personally I enjoyed them more than the gardens for – until the Second World War – they withstood the changes wrought by time and fashion and retained their pristine beauty. Moreover, the plantations improved with age.

There is a subtle difference between the parks and the "grounds" surrounding the principal dwellings. A further separation exists between them and the rest of the estate, which may be made up of agricultural land farmed by the landlord or leased to farming tenants. The traditional park is an area of open uncultivated grassland, a continuous unit, surrounded by a wall or fence. It lacks hedges, but contains carefully arranged clumps of trees, avenues and copses. There is generally a lake or stretch of water within the boundaries, often flanked by woodland and usually grazed by deer. It is, in fact, a quiet, private slice of open country enclosed for the exclusive use of the owner.

Waddesdon, Ascott and Exbury are situated in extensive grounds, in beautiful surrounding countryside, but they possess no classical park. The estates of Armainvilliers, Ferrières, Laversine and Schillersdorf included wonderful parks; in the days of Baron Edmond, that of Armainvilliers, designed by Eli Laîné, was particularly awe-inspiring and a great luxury; he employed 40 men to look after it. The banks and

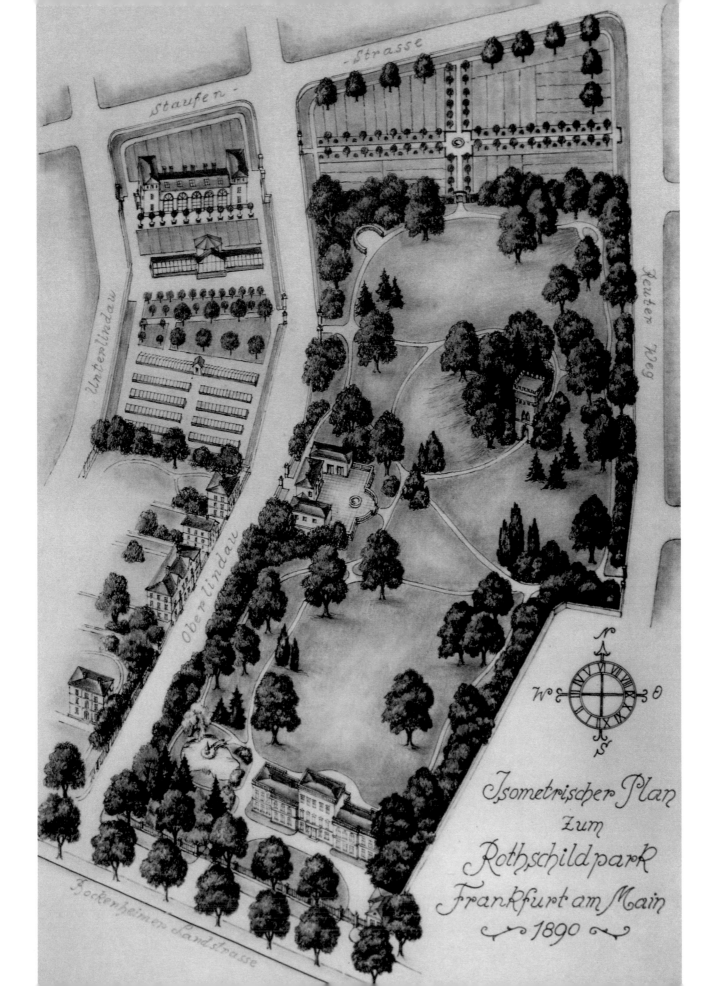

Staufen-

Strasse

Unterlindau

Oberlindau

Reuter Weg

Bockenheimer Landstrasse

N
W   O
S

Isometrischer Plan
zum
Rothschildpark
Frankfurt am Main
~ 1890 ~

surrounds of "100 hectares of calm water" were constructed by over 100 workmen. According to Marcel Gaucher (*see p. 28*), the soil was particularly suitable for the growth of tall trees and he described the park as "a prestigious arboretum". All the tree plantations were carefully thought out and arranged for form and colour, from the giant Californian *Sequoias* to the long avenue of local poplars. It was a work of art.

At Schillersdorf 350 acres were carved out of the estate (which included 11,000 acres of woodland), to make the park, and Baron Anselm employed over 100 workmen to excavate the large lake, which it was hoped would attract wild duck.

Neither Ferrières nor Laversine had classical gardens. The landscape, as Guy de Rothschild remarked, "originated at the foot of the terrace". Both owners, Edouard and Robert grew wonderful flowers and fruit in greenhouses and, like Edmond, kept the beehives within them. At Ferrières Edouard followed the family predeliction for orchids on which he lavished infinite care and attention. At Laversine (in 1932) 15 gardeners looked after individual hot houses each containing only a single species of flower. Two were reserved for grapes. Following the curious family whim of vegetables out of season, asparagus and green beans were forced for serving in February.

BELOW
View of the park at Ferrières

One of the attractions of Armainvilliers is the easy relationship of the house and the park. There are no terraces, walls or roads, unnatural "layout" or decorations between the building and the expanse of unhindered green and the shield of trees. An aerial photograph, however, showed how carefully the grass was mown in semi-circular waves to follow the contour of the front of the château. On the occasion of my last visit, wild boar had just begun to breed in the model farm and were about to be released in the park. Today the estate belongs to the King of Morocco and the fate of the wild boar remains uncertain.

A recent publication describes 57 town and country houses which the Rothschilds built or rebuilt in Europe. Each of these were provided with a garden, however small; at 148 Piccadilly it was barely the size of a tennis court, but its stone flower urns blazed with a delightful mixture of fuschias and lobelia. (It is hard to imagine them now lying as rubble beneath the ugly traffic of an expanded Park Lane.) However, only a few Rothschild houses were set in classical parks; altogether the family created and embellished perhaps a score, of which Paxton designed no less than five.

RIGHT
*Tring Park 1739: Charles Bridgeman's layout
and a number of buildings by James Gibbs -
engraving by Baddeslade*

TEN

Tring Park

There are more private parks in England than in any other country in Europe. In 1828 a German prince wrote enthusiastically to his wife that there were "at least a hundred thousand"[1] – possibly a slight exaggeration!

In 1087 thirty-one parks were recorded in England but between 1200-1350, the heyday of the mediaeval parks, the number had swelled to over 1900. They fulfilled two principal functions: first they provided a private surround to the manor house, and secondly an enclosure for deer and other farm animals, as well as game for the chase. The land enclosed was usually of poor agricultural quality but adequate for rough grazing. In 1596 Enfield Chase was described as a "solitarie desert yet stocked with 3,000 deer" and, at about the same period William Harrison[2] complained that "a twentyeth of the realm is employed upon deer and conies".

Tring Park in Hertfordshire was certainly the most beautiful and historically the most interesting of the Rothschild parks. The Manor of Trengues, which is mentioned in the Domesday Book, was at that time in the possession of Earl Eustace, Earl of Boulogne, whose daughter Mathilde married Stephen, King of England. Mathilde granted the Manor of Trengues to the Abbot and Monks of St. Saviour who in turn, in 1340, granted it to the Archbishop of Canterbury[3].

King James I in turn granted it to his eldest son, but after the death of the Prince it passed to his second son, Charles I, who settled it upon his Queen, Henrietta Maria in dower for 99 years. On her death it came into the possession of Henry Guy, Groom of the Bedchamber and Clerk of the Treasury during the reign of Charles II. It was he who paid Nell Gwyn her stipend and it was to "Elinors", a house within the Park, to which she

RIGHT
The obelisk standing at the centre of a star-shaped system of walks in Tring Park

probably returned when the plague was raging in London. According to Salmon[4] (1728) Henry Guy "had gardens of unusual Form and Beauty" round his house which was designed by Christopher Wren. The Park, however, was transformed by the son of Sir William Gore, Lord Mayor of London, who purchased the property from Henry Guy.

Even two hundred years ago main roads appear to have been a problem at Tring, for William Gore, before he began redesigning the gardens and its surroundings, diverted three quarters of a mile of the Icknield Way out of the Park! William Gore engaged Charles Bridgeman, a landscape gardener, and architect James Gibbs to create the 300 acre elaborate Baroque layout, well illustrated by Baddeslade's engraving (*see p. 140*). Bridgeman invented the ha-ha; it was suggested that by so doing he "had anticipated a major step in the evolution of park and garden" since it provided the sweep of an uninterrupted view of both. The longer of the two canals, which could be viewed from the front of the house, was 1,000 feet long by 100 feet wide, and the avenues which flanked it were each planted with 106 standard yews and 106 standard elms. Nine men and several boys looked after the garden.

Tring changed hands several times before Lionel de Rothschild, in 1872, bought the 4,000 acre estate which included the Manor and the Park, and a herd of 300 fallow deer, for a sum equivalent to eight million pounds today. He gave it to his eldest son "Natty" as an additional wedding present. In the meantime, one of the previous owners had swept away the formal gardens, drained the canals and broken up the avenues of trees, but the ha-ha remained. When repairing the deer fence along the bottom of the ditch, a gold guinea piece of Charles II's reign was turned up, and is now in my collection.

Emma Rothschild wrote to her mother-in-law when she first arrived in her new home, "Tring is fairyland ...". Fortunately Natty greatly appreciated the natural beauty of this piece of the Chiltern escarpment, and he had the good sense to leave the Park untouched. It was, however, maintained with meticulous care. He installed a nursery along the perimeter of Bull's Wood where he grew replacements for the trees lost by storm or old age. He also planted a remarkable collection of various species of conifers opposite Rangers Cottage; the grass rides between the rows were brightened with daffodils each spring. (This plantation was wrecked in the 1987 hurricane). Sheets of bluebells on the far side of the principal pathway, under the beech trees, were left to grow naturally. Apart from the team of skilled foresters and woodsmen, it was customary

ABOVE
Keys to King Charles' ride at Tring Park, and Ashton woodlands
RIGHT
"Natty" (Lord Rothschild), owner of Tring Park and described by the Daily News in 1908 as "the real ruler of England"
BELOW
Tring Park, with the flag of the Lord Lieutenant of the County flying, the ha-ha and emus
FOLLOWING PAGES
View of Tring Park and the distant Chiltern escarpment

to employ any inhabitant of Tring who wanted a job and firewood for their own use. It was small wonder the woods looked well cared for.

Tring Park has now been scheduled by the Countryside Commission as an area of outstanding natural beauty, encompassing two sites of Special Scientific Interest[5]. English Heritage included Tring in their register of parks and gardens of historic interest. Certainly no more beautiful spot could be found anywhere in England and the view from King Charles' Ride, along the escarpment, is unforgettable, with the background of massive beech trees – flaming orange and crimson in the Autumn – and the "easy"[6] chalk grassland hill below. In the distance, the Vale of Aylesbury is spread out in a peaceful emerald green patchwork beyond the tiny wedding-cake-like turrets of Mentmore. Charles Bridgeman's star-shaped system of woodland rides, with James Gibb's obelisk at the centre, and the portico of his Ionic Temple on the crest of Oddy Hill, still remain – but all badly in need of repair.

As children we spent every winter at Tring and we were convinced the obelisk was a memorial to Nell Gwyn's dog! I still treasure the key I was given to the gate leading onto King Charles' Ride, but in those days I thought the farm and woodlands just outside the park – Brown's Lane and Timberlake's Farm – even more delightful, because they were not so well manicured. But the steepsided chalk bluffs and dry valleys of the deer park were excellent for tobogganing and sledging, and I remember with nostalgia the hills deep in snow, the towering trees glittering with hoar frost and the rooks wheeling above them, cawing of unnumbered springs.

Natty made Tring Park famous with his agricultural activities, although his son Walter's kangaroos, emus and cassowaries which roamed the precincts, along with the deer and Reeves and Amherst pheasants, attracted more publicity. For Natty "improvement" and excellence were the salt of life and he concentrated on developing new practices and "improvements" to his animals and their management. He bred world-famous shorthorns, Jersey cows and shire horses, and sent stock to South Africa, Japan and the United States. He introduced electricity and an improved milk recording system into the dairy. Country Life remarked that "Tring Park was included in most itineraries drawn up for the guidance of foreign visitors on account of the high reputation for excellence of general management"[7].

I dimly recall the Agricultural Show held in the park – the tents, flags and a brass band – but more clearly the first sheepdog trials which were staged just beyond the ha-ha.

Natty planted a half mile avenue of lime trees immediately opposite Walter's Museum which he had built on the perimeter of the Park, as a birthday present for his eldest son. He was less fortunate with his remodelling in 1880 of the Manor House itself. It looked more imposing, but uninteresting – red brick with rows of large windows and a grey slate mansard roof which Jackson Stops described as "much in the French taste". Actually the Wren structure beneath the new facade could have easily been rescued. The octagonal cupola removed from one of James Gibbs' garden pavilions, which had been dismantled, was added to the stables and proved an unqualified success. As a schoolgirl, I longed to live in the stables!

Natty placed the kitchen garden, the hothouses and fruit frames, with accommodation for the head gardener and his staff, half a mile from the house. One of the greenhouses was set aside for flowers sent every year to Queen Mary on her birthday. The orchids Walter grew at Tring, and the crosses he produced were magnificent. He was one of the initial recipients of the Royal Horticultural Society's Victoria Medal of Honour.

Victor (3rd Lord Rothschild) inherited Tring Park when his grand-mother, Emma, died in 1935 and her life-interest in the house and its sur-roundings was extinguished. He and his wife remained there for a short trial period but he had no sentimental attachment to Tring, which was too grand for his taste, and he also felt unable to shoulder the heavy responsi-bility and sky-high tradition of the estate. He appreciated the fact that the Chiltern Hill escarpment was a landscape of national importance and fur-thermore that the Natural History Museum in London required addition-al storage room and working facilities; moreover the Trustees were also considering the transfer of the ornithological department to Walter's Museum[8], which they had recently acquired. He generously offered the Manor, its grounds and stables, including the Park and the woodlands, to the British Museum of Natural History as a gift.

The Committee appointed to consider this offer did not accept it. This showed an astonishing lack of judgement and was to prove very costly for the tax-payer, since new building on a large scale both in London and at Tring Museum, and a new store equipped at Wandsworth

RIGHT
Tring Park – the lime avenue in autumn

could have been avoided. With the Manor and stables, Walter Rothschild's Museum, the Chiltern escarpment and the Park, Tring could have been one of the most magnificent Natural History Museums in the world. It is also unlikely that a busy road would then have been constructed across the Park.

The death of Victor's grandparents, parents and uncle within the space of 25 years, and the consequences of the Second World War, drastically altered life at Tring, but yet another disaster threatened the Park. In 1953 the Ministry of Transport announced a proposal to construct a loop off the nearby main road, the A41, which was to cross Tring Park and pass within about 150 yards of the front of the Manor, diverting the heavy traffic from the town's High Street. A public enquiry was held and I was one of the many outraged objectors. At considerable expense counsel was engaged and an alternative route surveyed and proposed. The Ministry then withdrew the scheme. My legal adviser explained this was not a matter for rejoicing since the Ministry had not "lost the case" and would, in all probability resuscitate it within the next ten years. "And then," he added gloomily, "you will not be able to afford to fight them again."

Unfortunately his pessimism proved justified. In 1973 the same route was proposed again by the Ministry. This time the public enquiry lasted over three months. It was accurately described as "costly window-dressing". I conducted my own case and lent my counsel to the Tring Society. By now the alternative route had been partly built over and I knew ours was a lost cause. The bypass was constructed across the Park. Had Natty been alive he, like William Gore, would have been able to divert the road round Tring town. But we lacked the influence and the talent to save a designated area of outstanding natural beauty from this needless desecration.

Fortunately, the local authority* who recently purchased the Park has leased it to the Woodland Trust for 399 years, so there is hope that the crest of the ridge and the "easy" chalk hillocks, the sea of bluebells and the Chiltern Gentian will be saved from further destruction. And Gibb's obelisk, now flaking off at the base, will be repaired. Perhaps after all it is a monument to Nell Gwyn's dog?

FOOTNOTE
*Dacorum Borough Council

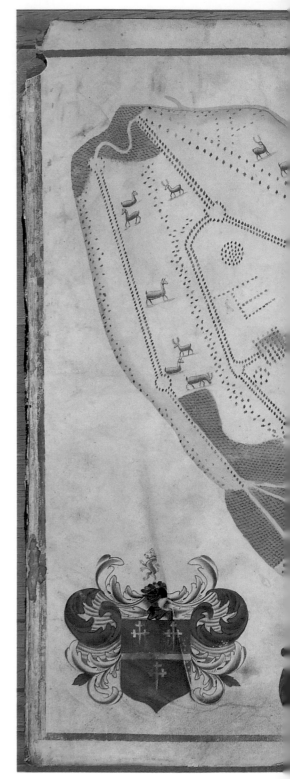

A map of Tring Park made for William Gore based on a survey of 1719

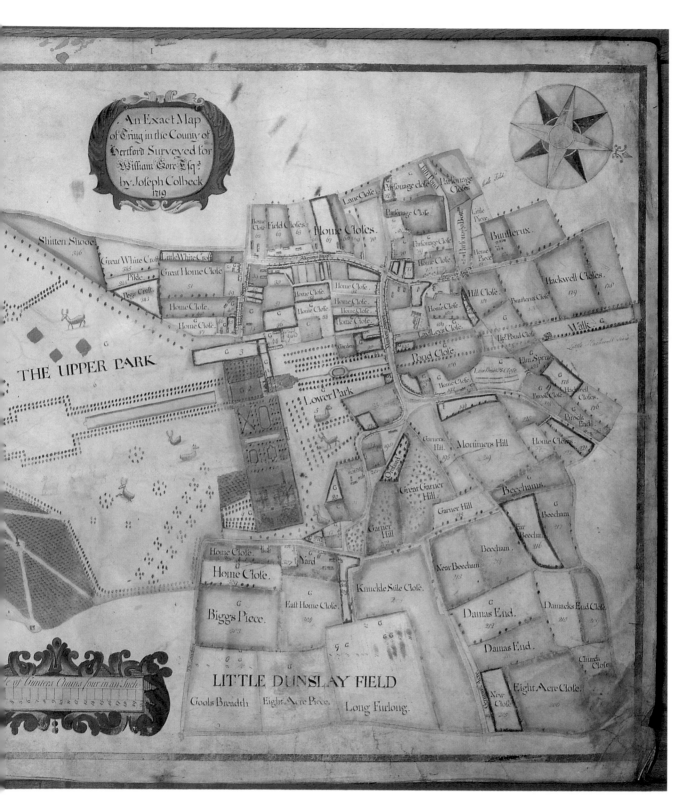

An Exact Map
of Tring in the County of
Hertford Surveyed for
William Gore Esq.ʳ
by Joseph Colbeck
1719

Shitten Shooe
346

Great White Croft
345
Pikle
344
Peggs Croft
343
Little White Croft
Great Home Close

Home Field Closes
65 64 65

Home Closes.
66 67 68 69 70

Lane Close
72

Parsonage close
73

Parsonage Close

Parsonage Closes

Butlerux

Hackwell Closes.
119 118

Home Close
51

Home Close.
49

Home Close.
37

Home Close
36

Home Close.
44

Home Close
32

Home Close
84

Home Close
Home Close.

Hill Close.
181

Home Piece

Home Close

Butlers Close

Home Close
180

Walk

THE UPPER PARK

Lower Park

Garden

Low Leys Close.

Pond Close
106

Home Close
193

Low Points Close
192

Home Close
194

Elm Spring
G

Hackwell
Brook Close

Hackwell
Closes.
176

Brook
End

Little Hackwell Steed

Oakland

Garners
Hill.
195

Mortimers Hill
249

Great Garner
Hill

Garner Hill
196

Garner
Hill

Beechams

Beecham
247

Far
Beecham
216

Home Close.
Home Close.
300

Yard

Bigg's Piece.
303

East Home Close.
304

Knuckle Stile Close.
2

Beecham
214

Near Beecham
213

Damas End.
212

Damas End.

Dammeks End Close
210   209

Church
Close

LITTLE DUNSLAY FIELD

Gools Breadth   Eight Acre Piece.   Long Furlong.

Near
Close
208

Eight Acre Close.
200

Scale of Gunters Chains four in an Inch

ELEVEN

Langau

Ferdinand de Rothschild (1839-1898) married an English cousin and decided to live in the Vale of Aylesbury (see Chapter Two). His brother, Salomon Albert, married a French cousin and decided to remain in Austria. He was a passionate botanist which may well have influenced him in his purchase in 1870 of a 30,000 hectare estate in the Kalkalpen mountains – the highest peak about 1,900 metres – and within 150 kilometres of Vienna[1]. It encompassed large areas of virgin forest, the Urwald, undisturbed since the Ice Age. This is the only woodland of such antiquity in central Europe and Langau is ecologically by far the most interesting and valuable Rothschild park, past or present.

Albert built the principal residence in the local style, with timber, a gabled roof and a white-plastered base. Nearby he constructed a mini-village in similar style, with houses for his 300 employees, a post office, inn, stables, storage barns, and workshops. Scattered about the woodlands were hunting lodges and wooden chalets.

Langau was magical. The mountain air truly produced an effect of fine wine. I first visited the place in August in late summer, in my teens. I found no walled garden round the house, no fence or hedge – suddenly it was *there*, with a narrow belt of brilliantly coloured zinnia planted just below the white walls. I noticed gaudy Jersey Tiger moths hanging like jewels from the flowers, nectaring in the sunshine. Opposite one end of the house was an icy stream falling over a pile of rocks into a shallow pool, with the sound of a mountain waterfall. I was suddenly conscious of a surge of light-hearted energy which was somehow connected with crystal clear air and brilliant altitude colours.

RIGHT
A view of the virgin forest
Taken from the booklet
Der Urwald Rothschild in den Niederösterreichischen Kalkalpen.

Verpflichtung:

INE EUROPÄISCHE VERANT

It was love at first sight for me. After about a week, I asked my cousin Alphonse, who had inherited half the estate from his father, if I could rent one of his empty chalets in the woods and study the forest community and the parasites of the Red deer, Roe deer, Chamois, Moufflon, badgers and foxes. He agreed at once, and suggested a rent of £4 per year! The Second World War extinguished the dream.

Albert, since one of his principal relaxations was shooting, released too many Red deer at Langau and they damaged the trees. The number of antlers and hunting trophies on the walls in the interior of the house was something which also jarred uncomfortably - a malaise of the times, and also a sign of social success! (The enormous "bags" of duck and game birds obtained at Tring shoots were a symptom of the same pleasure – of giving one's friends "a good time" and better sport than the neighbours could provide. This was a hundred years ago and fortunately times are changing. Culling is still a regrettable necessity, but at Ashton such "sport" is something forgotten – like cock fighting.)

Alphonse employed 190 men at Langau in the twenties, but his daughter Betty and her sister Gwen, who inherited the property, were obliged to reduce the numbers to 35. They and their parents were refugees from Nazi persecution and lived in the United States (where Alphonse died) from 1942-48. Langau was then occupied by the Russian army, but Betty and her mother regained possession of their home in 1953.

Unfortunately in Austria there is no state support or tax relief for landowners who manage and conserve areas of international scientific importance and interest. The Urwald with its precious forest community of animals and mountain flora, its giant trees up to 50 metres in height, its natural regeneration and awe-inspiring beauty, should be left inviolate. It is a living museum of the natural structure of the forest, and its owners should be financially supported in their efforts to preserve it. Today we are constantly reminded of the dangers threatening the tropical rain forests, but, sadly, nearer home this grandiose relic of the Ice Age is apparently forgotten.

ABOVE
Salomon Albert de Rothschild, a passionate botanist who selected the Kalkalpen mountains for his country residence

RIGHT
The Kalkalpen mountains
Taken from the booklet
Der Urwald Rothschild in den Niederösterreichischen Kalkalpen.

DAS ERBE BEWAHREN |

POSTSCRIPT

It is interesting to compare the chalets built by Albert at Langau for his employees with the cottages built at Ashton by Charles. The Langau chalets were constructed of local timber and the gabled roofs had a finish of slatted wooden tiles, while the cottages at Ashton were built of brick and local stone, and the roofs were thatched with reed and sedge. The English cottages had conventional gardens, with fruit trees at the back of each dwelling, and they were grouped round a large village green. The Austrian chalets were decorated with window boxes and were not set in separate gardens, but they had open grass parkland around them.

The inn at Ashton, the Three Horseshoes, was situated at the end of the green, and was originally licensed to sell wine and tobacco. When I became the landlady, I widened the license to include spirits as well as wine, and renamed the inn the Chequered Skipper, in honour of a rare local butterfly. For many years the bar exhibited a giant wax model of a flea, until one night revellers pulled off its legs. The inn – The Cabin – at Langau provided beer and sausages.

Ashton in 1901 was said to be the only village in England with a bath in every house. The Langau chalets were built in 1870 and wooden baths with a metal lining were installed in every one – thus Austria was thirty years ahead of us in this respect. Piped filtered water was provided for both villages. Classical porcelain-faced stoves were installed at Langau, while at Ashton cottages were heated by logs burnt in open fireplaces.

In those good old days, employees of the estates lived in the cottages and chalets rent and tax-free and remained in them after retirement or until they died. There was a Rothschild flavour about both these villages, although I doubt if the inhabitants knew of each other's existence.

RIGHT
The thatched inn at Ashton, named by the author the Chequered Skipper in honour of a local butterfly

BELOW
Chalets at Langau built at the foot of the mountains

TWELVE

Pregny

Adolph de Rothschild (1823-1900) first went to Geneva to consult a skilled ophthalmic specialist who successfully extracted a piece of metal which had lodged in his eyeball. In profound gratitude for the successful operation, he provided Geneva with a magnificent opthalmic hospital and foundation, and also decided to live permanently in this delectable canton. He therefore bought Pregny (in 1857) and made plans for building a château in the park. In order to supervise this project he purchased a piece of land between Pregny and the Lake of Geneva, where he erected a chalet and lived there with his wife until the château was finished.

Members of the Rothschild family possess a rather similar taste in houses, gardens and parks. This was partly dictated by the predilections of the time in which they lived and became wealthy. They had no long family history stretching back into the Middle Ages from which the Austrian, French and English branches could have diverged and diversified; after all, only one generation separated them from the Frankfurt ghetto. A further unifying factor in their *modus vivendi* and their taste was their compulsive emulation of one another.

Adolph originally intended to employ a well-known French architect Claret, and Varé a "decorative gardener" of the Bois de Boulogne, for Pregny. However, he eventually entrusted the task to Paxton (and his son-in-law George Stokes) who had built Mentmore, Ferrières and Aston Clinton and also laid out James de Rothschild's park at Boulogne. Furthermore, he employed Paxton to design his aviary, and to construct his magnificent glass range, 50 metres long with 15 minor houses opening into it. This covered more than a hectare of ground.

RIGHT
View over Lake Geneva from
the terrace at Pregny

OPPOSITE
View towards the château from the park

RIGHT
Julie, Baroness Adolph de Rothschild

BELOW
*The central covered walk
linking the greenhouses*

The park at Pregny with its hills and dales has a delightful light-hearted touch about it, quite unlike other Rothschild parks. This was originally due to Julie's influence, which filtered down the years. Julie, Adolph's cousin and wife, had a smudge of genius about her. Books about the family usually dwell only on the dinner she gave to the Empress Elizabeth the night before that tragic woman was assassinated. However, the Empress was a frequent visitor to Pregny, for she was enthralled by the wonderful display of flowers in the greenhouses. Julie, apart from her love of exotic plants, introduced amusing wild animals into the park and tropical birds into the aviary, and also planned the planting and arrangement of the gigantic trees. She realised the importance of the foreground contrasting with the distant view of the lake and snow-capped mountains, and managed to mix magnificence with the scent of flowering Swiss hay meadows.

In Baron Maurice's day (1950s) there was still a classical arrangement of Victorian *parterres*, like a necklace at the foot of the château itself, which were always planted with a dazzling display of conventional bedding-out plants. But they in no way impinged on the park. The vegetable garden and the splendid glasshouses were situated some distance away. Recently they were presented to the Jardin et Conservatoire Botanique of Geneva and are now being carefully restored.

Looking back to the times that I often visited Geneva I can remember distinctly how much I enjoyed the park at Pregny. Why should I recall the ducks on the water and the stretch of wild flowers in uncut grass so vividly? Or the tropical fish, now in the aviary? Or the brilliant autumn colours of the trees? I do not know, but strangely enough, quite apart from its self-contained beauty, Pregny emanates a contagious, most endearing, blithe spirit.

ABOVE
Map of the park and château at Pregny

RIGHT
Pollarded chestnut trees in the park

The Aftermath of War

The profound changes and the destruction wrought by two World Wars and the Nazi *régime* in Europe are almost unimaginable today. All the principal Rothschild gardens were lost in France, Austria and Germany, except for the Villa Ile de France.

When the younger members of the family were released from the army, and the older generation returned from their exile as refugees in England or America, the mood had undergone a drastic change in Europe and few found it possible to begin again at the beginning.

When Marcel Gaucher (*see p. 26*) returned to Boulogne from four years in a prisoner of war camp, he was so appalled at the devastation and wanton destruction in the park and garden that he turned and fled. Alexandrine immediately presented the property to the town of Boulogne and decided to live in Switzerland. Laversine was given to the French State by Robert de Rothschild. Alain and Elie, Robert's sons (who had also been prisoners of war in Germany), and their two sisters moved to smaller houses and soon designed delightful gardens. (At Royaumont today Elie employs three instead of 15 gardeners, and is himself a skilled and inventive "pruner"). Ferrières was donated to the University of Paris and Guy, the owner since his father's death, moved to the Château de Reux, the property willed to him by Beatrice Ephrussi's brother (*see p. 125*). The château had been occupied by the Germans, and the furniture and contents hurled out of the windows when they vacated the premises as the British Army landed on the French coast on D-Day. Armainvilliers was eventually sold.

In England Halton, Gunnersbury, Aston Clinton, Mentmore and Tring (after it was turned down by the British Museum) were sold. During the early years of the war, while I worked at Bletchley (*see p. 94*), I had the great good fortune to be billeted at Mentmore – sharing it with the crated Wallace collection[a], a nursery school and the Derby winner, Blue Peter[b]. I will never forget the huge lilac hedge, loaded with flowers, white, purple and various shades of mauve, which flanked the drive and the elegant bronze statue of King Tom[c] on the grass opposite – which put all the marble goddesses to shame.

RIGHT
All that remains near the site of the Villa Victoria, Alice de Rothschild's splendid Villa and gardens at Grasse, is this solitary tea house

Tring, Waddesdon, Mentmore and Halton shared matchless views of the Vale of Aylesbury – each one more beautiful than the next and all different – but for me there was something particularly moving in the valley below Mentmore. I confess I did not regret the lack of the impressive *parterres* on the terrace, but one knew in one's bones the war would destroy Mentmore.

Ascott and Waddesdon were accepted by the National Trust. Evelyn and his family continue to live at Ascott and Jacob and his family at Eythrope, but today only Ashton and Exbury remain with the grandchildren of the original creators and owners of Edwardian Rothschild gardens.

There are, however, additional reasons why these Rothschild gardens dwindled. By 1940 the family was about half the size it was in 1840 – simply there were fewer gardeners. Baron Ferdinand, the creator of Waddesdon, wrote in his Red Book[1]: "I fear that Waddesdon will share the fate of most properties that have no descendants and fall into decay. May the day yet be distant when weeds will spread over the gardens, terraces crumble into dust ...... and the melancholy cry of the nightjar sound from the deserted towers..."

Fortunately Ferdinand was too pessimistic about the fate of his gardens but – alas! – too optimistic about the nightjars.

FOOTNOTES

[a] *Wallace Collection, now at Portman Square, London*

[b] *In 1939*

[c] *A race horse, second in the Derby in 1954, despite suffering a severe illness*

RIGHT
The parterre at Mentmore before World War Two, after which it disappeared

LEFT
*The Theresianumgasse garden in Vienna,
which belonged to the Baron and Baroness
Alphonse, before World War Two. It was
completely destroyed during the Nazi régime*

BELOW
*The Ashton rose garden before World War
Two, with the Huckvale conservatory in the
background*

A Fortunate Juxtaposition

The period during which the Rothschilds were able to indulge in gardening on a grand scale exactly suited both their situation in Europe and their ebullient temperament. The classical Italian garden, the Elizabethan knot garden or the Capability Brown landscaped garden would have appealed to them far less. The Victorian and Edwardian epochs, with their exaggerated profusions of luxurious, colourful flowering plants and fruits, enormous hothouses full of palm trees, tropical ferns and exotic epiphytes, their formal *parterres* and clipped hedges alongside carefully mown lawns, stone and marble statues, fountains, pools and the excitement of collectors returning from distant countries with new species, and last but not least the revolutionary techniques for the production of delicious fruit and novel varieties of vegetables – were just their ideal style of gardening, infinitely satisfying with scope for creative planning.

The family exhibited all the traits associated with ardent collectors – ambition, enthusiasm, energy, possessiveness, the tireless acquisition of relevant information, and a mastery of detail. They were all lucky to share another useful quality - the ability to select the right man to put in charge of their enterprise, be it a museum, a gold refinery, a shipping company or a garden. Walter Rothschild, at the age of 24 chose two then unknown young men, of German nationality, to manage the Ornithological and Entomological departments of his future museum. Both became eminent zoologists - one was later described as "one of the great biological thinkers of our time". Baron Edmond decided that Marcel Gaucher (*see p. 26*), then aged 22, would make a good head gardener at Armainvilliers, where he would be in charge of a staff of 40, and Alice picked Johnson for Waddesdon when he was a trainee with only eighteen months practical experience. Head hunting was unnecessary!

The Rothschilds were successful gardeners, not simply because they fitted in so well with the nineteenth century European horticultural scenario, but because they also achieved the right balance between a keen narcissistic desire for approval and admiration, and a passionate love of plant life linked to an aesthetic appreciation of trees, fruits and flowers.

RIGHT
Spring bedding at Eythrope

LEFT
Statue of Eros at Ascott

RIGHT
*Geraniums, verbena and tobacco plants mingle
with more exotic plants in urns at Eythrope*

BELOW
Sweet williams make a colourful display

Rothschild Flowers
Species and Cultivars

The way in which the botanical names of plants are continually changing is confusing and irritating for all concerned. This is due to frequent alterations in the status of some species. Thus a so-called "good" species may turn out to be merely a variety, or a "sport" or a cultivar or even a cross between two other species – all of which lead to name changes. We have tried to avoid a muddle and have in most cases followed the names used in the *Royal Horticultural Society's Dictionary of Gardening* (2nd Edition)[1] but some of the most recent alterations may have been missed. Fortunately, it is still true that a flower smells as sweet by any name!

Around the turn of the century, it was well known that the Rothschild gardeners were keen collectors and growers of tropical orchids. Among them my uncle Walter (the second Lord Rothschild) was a "museum botanist" as well as a successful horticulturalist, and my father, his brother Charles, not only knew his plants but was a gifted collector and field naturalist. It is curious that neither of these entomologists studied the extraordinary relationship between insects and orchids. Although one species, named after Walter, had male and female flowers growing on different sprays of the same plant, he did not investigate their pollination. It fell to others to discover, for instance, that male and female bees of the same species are attracted to, and pollinate, different species of orchids. At least seven members of this family were named in honour of Rothschild gardeners.

RIGHT
Paphiopedilum rothschildianum, a species named in honour of Ferdinand de Rothschild, described as the most spectacular species in the genus

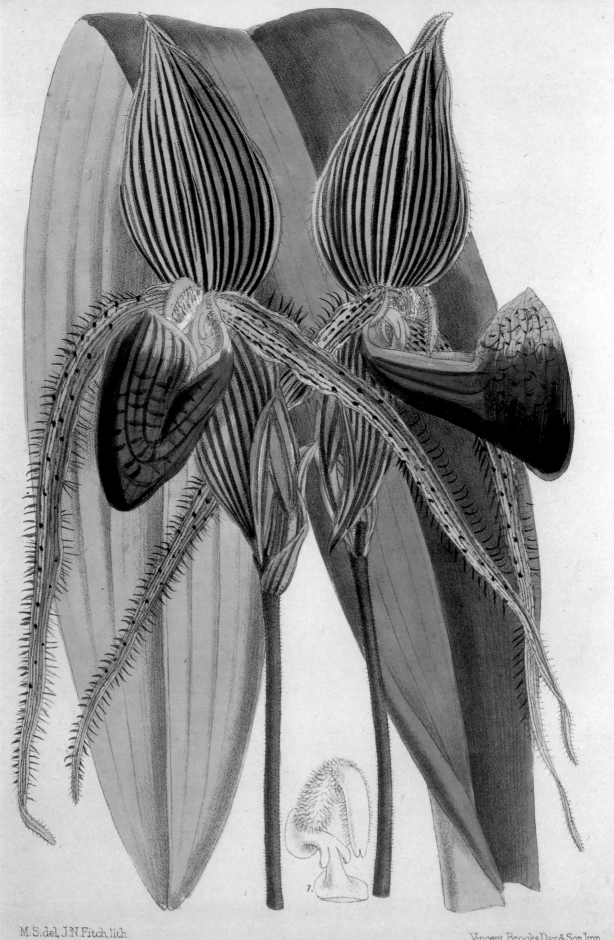

M.S.del, J.N.Fitch.lith.

Vincent Brooks Day & Son, Imp.

L.Reeve & Co. London.

Rothschild Species:

Paphiopedilum rothschildianum was described as *Cypripedium rothschildianum* by H.G. Reichenbach (1888), transferred to *Paphiopedilum* by Stein (1892), and named after Baron Ferdinand de Rothschild. This extremely rare orchid is endemic to the lower slopes of Mount Kinabalu in Borneo, and probably only survives because it is found in the Kinabalu Park, where it is protected from logging, mining, agriculture and, hopefully, from collectors. It is pollinated by Syrphid flies which are lured by the resemblance of its glandular staminate hairs to aphids, on which the larvae normally prey after hatching. While ovipositing the female becomes smothered in pollen and the next similar visit to another flower will affect cross-pollination and fertilisation.

P. *rothschildianum* is described as the most spectacular species in the *genus*; the flowers are very large (30 centimetres in diameter) with glossy green leaves and petals "yellow and ivory white marked with maroon". Reichenbach considered it "one of the most astonishing introductions we have ever seen". This species has been extensively used for the production of hybrids.

Ancistrochilus rothschildianus (O'Brien 1907) is a West African epiphyte collected for Walter Rothschild in Nigeria; it flowered at Tring and he immediately arranged for W.G. Smith to draw it from life. Those were the days before easy photography! It has unusually large, pink and white flowers with a brown blotch on the lip.

Angraecum rothschildianum (O'Brien 1903) is a fragrant epiphyte described as a "charming plant from Uganda". It was discovered in 1878 in the environs of Victoria Nyanza by Major H.B. Rattray of the King's African Rifles while exploring "new country". It is now called *Eurychone rothschildiana* [(O'Brien) Schlechter 1918]. This orchid belonged to a section never before introduced into gardens. It flowered at Tring Park and was awarded a botanical certificate by the R.H.S. in 1902 and named in honour of Walter Rothschild.

Cirrhopetalum rothschildianum (O'Brien 1895) is a spectacular orchid, bright purple with yellow markings, originally collected "somewhere in the hills beyond Darjeeling" for Walter Rothschild

ABOVE
Walter Rothschild: fourteen species and subspecies of plants were named in his honour including five orchids and the Flame lily

Vanda Rothschildiana, a hybrid orchid
produced by a Rothschild gardener and named
in honour of Walter Rothschild

The Queen's profile on a 33p stamp honours
this beautiful violet-blue orchid
Reproduced by permission of the
British Post Office

Vanda Rothschildiana

1993©

33

and named in his honour. It was reared with immense trouble at Tring, where it flowered in 1895 and received a first class certificate from the Orchid Committee of the R.H.S. (It was transferred to *Bulbophyllum* by J.J. Smith in 1912).

Catasetum rothschildii (Rolfe 1922) was collected for Walter Rothschild, in whose honour it was named. It flowered at Tring in 1899. It is remarkable for the morphological difference between male and female flowers which are borne on separate spikes. The flowers are light green with the inside of the lip buff yellow.

Cattleya rothschildiana was a natural hybrid between *Laelia lobata* and *Cattleya intermedia*. It was described from Brazil in 1882 as *Laelia amanda* and *C. rothschildiana* is now named *Laeliocattleya* x *amanda*.

Vanda Rothschildiana: this beautiful plant with violet-blue flowers, chequered with darker markings, is a hybrid produced artificially by Chassaing, the head-gardener at Ferrières, in 1931 and named in honour of Walter (the 2nd Lord Rothschild). It was registered at that time as a cross between *V. coerulea* and *V. sanderiana*.

Rosa rothschildii (Druce 1913) was discovered by Clarence Druce at Ashton Wold, while visiting Charles; the two men enjoyed various collecting expeditions together. This bright pink rose was, at one time, thought to be a variety of *Rosa tormentella* and later a variety of *Rosa obtusifolia*, but some experts have now decided it is a hybrid of *Rosa canina* and *Rosa sherardii*, but can retain the original name of *Rosa rothschildii*. It is obviously a very "difficult" genus!

Iris rothschildii (Von Degen 1936) was thought to be a natural hybrid between *Iris illyrica* and *Iris variegata*. Von Degen and Charles collected together extensively in Hungary. The former wrote in an obituary notice that Charles "had passed the line which separated collectors from scientists"; he admired his "extraordinary thorough knowledge of natural history" and described him as the "most amiable and straightforward character I have ever met".

Rumex rothschildia (Aaronsohn and Evanari 1940) was named in honour of Baron Edmond de Rothschild who founded numerous agricultural settlements in Israel (*see Chapter Six, Ramat Hanadiv*). It is a rare dock found on the sand dunes along the coastline in Israel. I was once "botanising" with Tamar Mendelssohn in this area when I found a modest unprepossessing plant which I did not recognise and showed it to my companion. She shook her head and consulted her handbook. "Believe it or not", she exclaimed, "it's a Rothschild!"

RIGHT
The climbing Flame lily, Gloriosa rothschildiana, a toxic plant named in honour of Walter Rothschild

Gloriosa rothschildiana (O'Brien 1903): the brilliant scarlet Flame lily is one of the most beautiful flowers named in honour of Walter Rothschild. This tropical African plant climbs by means of the tendril-like terminal portion of its leaves. The fleshy tubers are especially poisonous, but all portions of the plant contain toxins. When the flowers first open, the tips of the petals meet in the centre, then lash backwards like the ears of a vicious horse, but gradually assume a more classical tigerlily-like conformation. If sprays of the plant are cut and placed in an arrangement in a vase, the flowers work their way to the outside of the bunch – presumably they are attracted to the light – and arrange themselves like candles on a Christmas Tree.

Gloriosa rothschildiana is now assumed to be a variety of *G. superba*. The variety we grew at Ashton for 60 years (until a freak frost destroyed all our tubers, which were stored in sand for the winter in the basement of my house) was not like the *Gloriosa rothschildiana* now available from horticultural centres, or those exhibited at flower shows. Our variety had much stiffer, crisper petals and their yellow margins crimped, with the so-called "waves" much closer together. This plant flowered more profusely than the current form, which also has relatively limp petals tending to spread outwards. It has been suggested that a separate family, *Colchicaceae* should be erected for *Gloriosa*.

The late Sir John Fryer* told me that he was once sent to investigate a series of mysterious deaths which had occurred in Sri Lanka. He found that scrapings of the tubers of *Gloriosa rothschildiana* had been, perhaps deliberately, introduced into a cauldron of otherwise excellent soup. Death was probably due to colchicine, one of the poisonous alkaloids found in the plant. The Zulus are said to use the powdered tubers to increase sexual potency – but this quality is claimed for a remarkable number of African plants. A tropical caterpillar eats the leaves of *Gloriosa* but when half grown

ABOVE
Anthurium 'Rothschildianum',
a hothouse cross made by F. Bergman, the
Rothschild gardener at Ferrières, now
considered a variety of A. scherzerianum

changes to finish its development on a less toxic plant. By then it has probably stored enough poisons to protect it from bird predators.

Anthurium 'Rothschildianum' (1876) belongs to a tropical South American genus. It is now considered a variety of *A. scherzerianum* which originally came from Costa Rica. The spathe is shiny, sealing-wax red, sometimes with a few white spots and the cylindrical, twisted yellow spadix carries a number of minute, perfect flowers.

The Waddesdon gardens won a gold medal at the Chelsea Flower Show in 1928 with a spectacular collection of *Anthurium*. The majority of these plants had the erect not twisted spadix, (vaguely reminiscent of an erect penis), but it was shortly before the everyday appearance of the pale pink and pure white spathe. *Anthurium* are typically tropical in spirit and yet one imagines they cannot really be flowers... Several sub-varieties of *A.* 'Rothschildianum' have been described and named.

Rhododendron rothschildii (Davidian 1972) was named after Lionel de Rothschild (Exbury). Found by Rock in Yunnan in 1929, this good species is thought by some to have originated as a natural hybrid. The wild plant grows about 20 feet high but in cultivation it is a rounded nine foot shrub. The trusses contain 12 - 17 pale creamy-white or pale yellow flowers with a crimson blotch at the base. In bud they are deep crimson purple.

Rothschild Cultivars:

A glance at any gardeners' catalogue suggests that horticulturalists as a whole decided to flatter the Rothschilds with roses. This is rather curious because, although the whole family grew these matchless decorations, none of us were rose specialists. Nevertheless, we must be pleased with 'Baron' and 'Baroness Rothschild', 'Baronne Rothschild', 'Baron Edmond' and 'Baron Adolph'.

'Baroness Rothschild' is featured in Peter Beales Roses. It is a seductive large hybrid tea rose and is said to have "soft clear rose pink petals with a soft silky texture highly scented... – the bush is covered with large grey green foliage."

At Exbury the owners, past and present, have affectionately named many of their best cultivars after members of the family. There are various exquisite cymbidium varieties some of which received awards – 'Rozsika' (my mother), 'Nathaniel' (my grandfather), 'Mrs Lionel de Rothschild' and so on and on; they qualified as "among the top quality orchids of post war years."

The rhododendron cultivars followed the same pattern. At least a score are named after Lionel's relatives. After his death a first rate garden hybrid which he raised received an F.C.C: "Dresden yellow, crimson blotch and crimson spotting in the throat, carries 18 flowers on a truss", it was named by his son 'Lionel's Triumph'. Anthony Waterer raised an award of merit rhododendron cultivar, "white flushed blush pink and spotted crimson" which he called 'Lady de Rothschild'. Van Houtte, over a hundred years ago, raised an azalea "rich purple and pale violet double flowered" which he named 'Baron Nathaniel de Rothschild' and which received two first class certificates.

ABOVE
Cotoneaster 'Exburiensis'
a popular cultivar raised by
Lionel de Rothschild

Perhaps the best known family cultivars are *Cotoneaster* 'Rothschildianus', and *C.* 'Exburiensis'. Both are hybrid crosses of *C. frigidus* 'Fructuluteo' and *C. salicifolius*. The former has lemon-yellow and the latter golden-yellow berries. They are grown extensively in England.

There is also a violet named in honour of Baroness Alice (her favourite flower) which appeared in her garden as a seedling in 1894. A very similar variety was sold under the name of 'Baron Louis de Rothschild'. A camellia was named in honour of Charlotte de Rothschild, a nerine for Kate, a pelargonium for Baron Alphonse de Rothschild, and a begonia and carnation for Mrs Leopold de Rothschild.

There are also Rothschild "ghost" cultivars which sway in and out of magazine articles or appear in letters or in discussions, or even in photographs, but which do not really seem to exist. *Odontoglossum* Armainvillierense was one of the early *odontoglossum* crosses and caused great excitement; indeed Leroy, the gardener at Armainvilliers, is credited with being "the first to hybridise this most beautiful and interesting genus", producing *O.* Wilckeanum 'Leroyanum' (1891). A "magnificent variety", *O.* Wilckeanum 'Rothschildianum', pale yellow with heavy brown blotches, was dedicated to Ferdinand by Sander. Sander dedicated *Cattleya* Lord Rothschild to Natty, which was responsible for an astonishing 55 primary crosses up to 1946. Finally, Veitch dedicated his second ever *Phalaenopsis* cross (1887), *P.* Rothschildiana, to Natty, "one of the most enthusiastic lovers and collectors of *Phalaenopsis*": described as white with sepals flushed pale sulphur-yellow and with purple spotting on the lip, it too echoes down the years but seems strangely elusive.

ABOVE
R. 'Lionel's Triumph', a rhododendron hybrid named in honour of Lionel de Rothschild who made the cross shortly before his death

FOOTNOTE
Sir John Fryer 1886 - 1948: Botanist; plant pathologist; entomologist to the Board of Agriculture

Bibliography

Unless otherwise indicated, the references that follow refer to points specifically annotated in the text

Chapter One: A Passion for Gardening *pp.12-29*
1. Lucas Phillips, C.E. and Barber, P.N: *The Rothschild Rhododendrons*, revised ed. Cassell, London 1979
2. Rothschild, Miriam: *The Rothschilds and the original E.E.C.* Apollo, April 1994 *pp.7-13*
3. Letters in the Rothschild Archive, London
4. Wilson, E.O: *On Human Nature*, Bantam Press, London 1979 and Harvard University Press, Cambridge, Mass., 1978 (paperback 1988)
5. Catalogue of orchids grown by Baroness de Rothschild at Gunnersbury Park
6. Prevost-Marcilhacy, Pauline: *Les Rothschild bâtisseurs et mécènes*, Flammarion, Paris 1995
7. Gaucher, Marcel: *Les Rothschild, Côté Jardins,* Privately printed, Paris 1982
8. Rothschild, Miriam*: Dear Lord Rothschild: Birds, Butterflies & History*, Balaban Publishers, Pennsylvania 1983
9. Rothschild, Miriam: *The Silent Members of the First E.E.C: Family Reflections II: The Women...*(Ed. Georg Heuberger)
The Rothschilds: Essays on the History of a European Family, pp.155-164, Boydell and Brewer, New York 1994

Chapter Two: Waddesdon Manor *pp.32-47*
1. Elliott, Dr. Brent: *The History and Restoration of Waddesdon Manor Gardens 1874-1995,* The National Trust and Royal Horticultural Society Lecture, London, July 1995
2. Rothschild, Mrs James de: *The Rothschilds at Waddesdon Manor*, Collins, London 1979
3. Blunt, Anthony: *Destailleur at Waddesdon*, Apollo, June 1977 *pp.409-415*

Chapter Three: Exbury by Lionel de Rothschild *pp.48-71*
The following references are general works containing interesting information about Exbury and Gunnersbury
• Lucas Phillips, C.E and Barber, P.N:*The Rothschild Rhododendron*s, revised ed.

Cassell, London 1979

• Holland, A.J. and de Rothschild, E.L: *Our Exbury,* Paul Cave Publications, Southampton 1982

• Harper, Martin: *Mr Lionel: An Edwardian Episode*, Cassell, London 1970

• Articles by Lionel de Rothschild, and articles about Exbury in the *Journal of the Royal Horticultural Society*, *The Rhododendron Society Note*s, *The Year Book of the Rhododendron Association*, *The Rhododendron Year Book*, *The Garden*, *New Flora and Silva*, *The Spectator* and *Country Life*.

• Collett-White, Ann and James: *Gunnersbury Park and the Rothschilds,* Heritage Publications, London 1993

• Articles about Gunnersbury, or by J. Hudson and A. Bedford, gardeners at Gunnersbury, in *The Gardener's Chronicle, The Garden, The Journal of the Royal Horticultural Society* and *Country Life*

• Templewood, Viscount*: The Unbroken Thread,* Collins, London 1974

Chapter Four: Ascott *pp.72-81*

1. Bacon, Francis: *Essays*, Macmillan, London 1958
2. Hellyer, A.G.L: *A Garden of Strong Contrasts,* Country Life, 18 March 1976 *pp.662-664*

Chapter Five: Ashton Wold *pp.82-107*

1. Clare, John: 'Summer Happiness' in *The Midsummer Cushion*, Eds Anne Tibble and R.K.R.Thornton, Mid-Northumberland Arts Group in association with the Carcanet Press, Manchester 1979
2. Shelley, Percy Bysshe: 'Adonais' LII *p.487, The Complete Poetical Works of Shelley,* Ed. Hutchinson, Clarendon Press, Oxford 1904

Chapter Six: Ramat Hanadiv *pp.108-115*

1. Schama, Simon*: Two Rothschilds and the Land of Israel,* Collins, London 1978
2. Society for the Protection of Nature in Israel Research Report 1990: Breeding Birds of Ramat Hanadiv
3. Society for the Protection of Nature in Israel Research Report 1990: The Ecology and Biology of the Mountain Gazelle (*Gazella Gazella*) in Ramat Hanadiv

Chapter Seven: Ile de France *pp.118-125*

1. *The Villa Ephrussi de Rothschild:* Special Issue brochure by Beaux Arts Magazine, Publications Nuit et Jour, Paris 1993

Chapter Nine: Rothschild Parks *pp.136-141*
1. Prévost-Marcilhacy, Pauline: *Les Rothschild bâtisseurs et mécènes,* Flammarion, Paris 1995

Chapter Ten: Tring *pp.142-151*
1. Lasdun, Lady Susan: *The English Park: royal, private and public,* André Deutsch, London 1991 and The Vendome Press, New York, 1992
2. Clutterbuck, Robert: *The History and Antiquities of the county of Hertford,* Vol I, Nichols, Son & Bentley, London 1815
3. Cussans, J.E: *History of Hertfordshire 1879-1881*
4. Salmon, N: *History of Hertfordshire,* 1728
5. Register of Parks and Gardens of Special Historic Interest in England, English Heritage 1987
6. Jackson-Stops, Gervase: *Tring Park, Hertfordshire,* Country Life 25 November 1993, *pp.60-63*
7. Rothschild, Miriam: *Dear Lord Rothschild: Birds, Butterflies & History,* Balaban Publishers, Pennsylvania 1983, *p.315*
8. Everett, Nigel: *The Tory View of Landscape,* Yale University Press, New Haven & London 1994
9. Rothschild, Miriam: *Dear Lord Rothschild: Birds, Butterflies & History,* Balaban Publishers, Pennsylvania 1983, *p.211*

Chapter Eleven: Langau *pp.152-157*
1. Mayer, Hannes et al: *Der Urwald Rothschild in den Niederösterreichischen Kalkalpen,* Verein zum Schutz der Bergwelt

Chapter Twelve: Pregny *pp.158-163*
1. Corti, Count Egon Caesar: *The Reign of the House of Rothschild,* trans. Lunn, B & B, Gollancz, London 1928

The Aftermath of War *pp.164-169*
1. Baron Ferdinand de Rothschild's Red Book (unpublished diary)

Appendix: Rothschild Flowers: *pp.174-183*
1. *The Royal Horticultural Society Dictionary of Gardening,2nd edition,* Ed. Chittenden, Fred J. & Synge, Patrick M, Clarendon Press, Oxford, 1981
2. Beales, Peter: *Roses,* Harper Collins, London, 1982

Index

Where sub-headings are listed without page numbers, refer to main entries.
Numbers in *italics* indicate illustrations

PHOTOGRAPHIC CREDITS
All original colour plates and photographs are © the photographers, the lenders or the Collections. The cover and 39 additional colour photographs were taken by Andrew Lawson, 25 by Lionel de Rothschild, four for Chapter 6 by Shai Ginot and eleven by Miriam Rothschild. The back cover photograph was taken by Tony Evans. Single colour photographs were supplied by Paul Grover, Johan Wallaert, Baron Guy de Rothschild, Eric Crichton and the late Eric Hosking. Other colour plates came from the Royal Collection, the Royal Horticultural Society, and the Royal Mail. Colour photographs for Chapter Eleven, Langau, were supplied by Bettina Looram from the booklet *Der Urwald Rothschild in den Niederösterreichischen Kalkalpen.*

Single black and white original photographs were taken by Ruth Ivor, the late Clarisse von Wertheimstein and Katherine Hahn while Robert Cotton copied a great variety of black and white photos from different sources past and present.

Andrew Lawson took the photographs on pages 4, 8, 13, 21, 22 below, 25, 29, 30, 33, 37, 43, 46, 47, 57, 58 above, 73, 74, 77, 79 below, 80 below, 81, 83, 84, 92, 100, 101 below, 102, 105, 134, 143, 147, 149, 157 above, 171, 173, 172 below, 179, 180, 182.

Miriam Rothschild took the photographs on pages 15 above, 35, 39 left, 41, 88, 89, 90, 96, 101 top, 103, 104.

Lionel de Rothschild took the photograph on the front cover and those on pages 49, 55, 56, 58 below, 59, 61, 63, 65, 67, 68, 69, 71, 116, 119, 121, 122, 123, 124, 159, 161, 163, 165, 183.

Shai Ginot took the photographs on pages 109, 111, 113, 115; that on page 38 was taken by the late Eric Hosking.

Paul Grover took the photograph on page 10, Eric Crichton the top photograph on page 177 and Johan Wallaert the photograph on page 99. The Royal Collection at Windsor supplied the plate on page 19; Beth Rothschild the plan on page 45; the Royal Horticultural Society supplied plates on pages 52 and 175; the Royal Mail the lower plate on page 177. Guy de Rothschild supplied photographs on pages 138 and 139.

Katherine Hahn took the photograph on page 85 above; Clarisse von Wertheimstein page 85 below; Ruth Ivor page 169. The photograph on page 23 was supplied by Bob Grace; on page 133 by Hans Dieter Eisterer. The Rothschild Archive supplied the photograph on pages 24 and and the original Family Tree to amend; the National Monuments Record supplied photographs on pages 130 below, 167 and 172 above.

The plan on page 80 came with kind permission of Arabella Lennox-Boyd; that on page 110 from The Rothschild Foundation, Jerusalem. The map on page 162 and photograph 160 below came from Edmond de Rothschild; the engraving on page 140 came from Country Life; the map on page 137 was supplied by the Institut für Stadtgeschichte in Frankfurt.

Photographs on pages 51, 53, 64, 78, 79 above and 145 were supplied by Lionel de Rothschild, taken by his grandfather; those on pages 50 and 66 were also supplied by Lionel de Rothschild.

All other photographs were supplied by Miriam Rothschild, or came from private Collections.

PUBLISHER'S ACKNOWLEDGEMENTS

Editor: Charlie Ryrie
Designer: Sara Mathews
Art Direction: Patrick Nugent
Production: Jim Pope

Gaia Books would like to thank all those who have generously supplied photographs and archive material for consideration and inclusion. We greatly regret that space did not permit us to include more. We would also like to thank all who have helped in research and fact-checking.

Thanks also go to Hannah Wheeler, Jan Dunkley and Tamsin Juggins at Gaia Books for their administrative support.